The Ultimate Unofficial

CONTENTS

Introduction

This book was started back in 2018, but it took two years and a pandemic for me to get off my backside and finish it.

When I resumed work on this project in March, 2020, I decided that a goodly chunk of any earnings I make from it should go to charity. I'm therefore happy to confirm that half of my income from this book will go to charity.

Details of the charities that have benefited will be posted from time to time on my website: www.thelosthighway.online.

In the meantime, please accept my thanks for purchasing this book. I hope that you enjoy it.

Finally, a word or two about copyright.

As per its title, this book is not an official product of either Formula One Management Limited or the Federation International de l'Automobile, nor is it endorsed by them.

The terms 'Formula One', 'F1', 'Grand Prix' and 'Formula One Grand Prix' are the trademarked property of Formula One Licensing BV. All other trademarks mentioned within the pages of this book are the property of their respective owners.

About this book

It seems appropriate to start with a question, so here's one to ponder: 'When is a quiz book not a quiz book?'

When it's a history book as well.

To explain: there are nineteen multiple choice sections, each containing ten questions, plus a section containing eleven questions. So far, so quiz book.

But where this book differs from other quiz books is that for every multiple-choice question there's a story that contains facts, statistics and/or trivia that relates to the question, the answer to it, or both. So it's a history book (of sorts) as well as a quiz book.

With that out of the way, there are some other points to which I'd like to draw your attention.

This version of the book does not, alas, include the excellent illustrations provided by Marcus Ward that feature in the Ebook version. Unfortunately, the cost of printing in colour was prohibitively expensive.

All is not lost, however, as examples of Marcus's work can be seen at (and copies can be purchased from) his redbubble store: redbubble.com/people/marcustward/shop

By way of compensation, this version of the book includes some additional questions, those in list-type format, which should test the knowledge of even the most ardent F1 fan.

As with all books, the contents of this one are fixed at a specific point in time. Some of the answers to the questions in the book will change over time – indeed, some already have. When playing the quiz, please bear in mind that, unless otherwise stated, the answers to the questions are accurate (I hope…) as at the end of 2019.

Please also be aware that in this book the terms 'F1' and 'Grand Prix' refer to the Formula One World Championship and the races of which it is composed. I mention this because in days of yore the term 'Grand Prix' was frequently used to describe non-championship F1 races and, indeed, races that were not run to F1 rules and often did not feature F1 cars.

And whilst we're talking about terms used to describe racing championships, I have taken the liberty of using the word 'IndyCar' as a generic term for the various incarnations of the USA's premier open-wheel racing series.

Which leads us nicely to the Indianapolis 500. From 1950 to 1960, the Indy 500 counted towards the F1 world championship. As it was run to different rules from the other rounds of the championship, it was not regarded as a Grand Prix nor as an F1 race. And that's how it has been treated in this book.

David M. Milloy
August, 2020

Part One: The Questions

In this part of the book, you'll find two types of questions designed to put your knowledge of F1 to the test.

As in the Ebook version, there are 201 multiple choice questions. As stated above, these are split into 19 sections of ten plus one section of eleven.

The first seven sections deal with the history of F1 from 1950 to date, there being one question for every year of its existence. Next up is seven general knowledge sections, followed by two sections about F1 drivers, two on the teams, and finally two on some of the more unusual events to have happened in F1 over the last 70 years.

The stories that relate to the multiple-choice questions and/or their answers can be found in Part Three of the book.

The multiple-choice questions are followed by twelve list-type questions. These are unique to the paperback version and cover a variety of topics, from 1950s Grand Prix winners to drivers who won world championships with more than one team.

Before you set about tackling the questions, it seems only right to give you a friendly warning: if you think you know everything there is to know about F1 then be prepared to think again!

Have fun.

1950

Which circuit hosted the first ever Formula One Grand Prix?

A.   Monaco

B.   Silverstone

C.   Monza

D.   Spa

1951

In how many Grands Prix were podium finishes achieved by non-Italian cars?

A.   Six

B.   None

C.   Four

D.   Two

1952

Who missed the entire 1952 Formula One season through injury?

A.   Nino Farina

B.   Alberto Ascari

C.   Juan Manuel Fangio

D.   José Froilán González

1953

Which Grand Prix became the first true fly-away Grand Prix in 1953?

A.   Brazilian

B.   Canadian

C.   South African

D.   Argentinian

1954

Alberto Ascari drove for Ferrari, Lancia and which other team in 1954?

A.   Mercedes

B.   Vanwall

C.   Maserati

D.   Gordini

1955

At which circuit did Stirling Moss notch his first Grand Prix victory?

A.   Aintree

B.   Brands Hatch

C.   Oulton Park

D.   Silverstone

1956

Peter Collins gave up his championship chances by doing what at Monza?

A.   He withdrew from the race

B.   He handed over his car to Fangio

C.   He allowed Fangio to pass him

D.   He deliberately incurred a time penalty

1957

Which circuit became the longest ever to be used for a Grand Prix?

A.   Nürburgring, Germany

B.   Porto, Portugal

C.   Pescara, Italy

D.   Sebring, USA

1958

In this year, who became the first British world champion?

A.   Stirling Moss

B.   Graham Hill

C.   Mike Hawthorn

D.   Tony Brooks

1959

Who scored BRM's first Grand Prix win?

A.   Graham Hill

B.   Dan Gurney

C.   Giancarlo Baghetti

D.   Jo Bonnier

1960

Who scored the first Grand Prix victory for Lotus as a constructor?

A.　　Jim Clark

B.　　Innes Ireland

C.　　Stirling Moss

D.　　John Surtees

1961

What was unique (at the time) about the 1961 Dutch Grand Prix?

A.　　It was held in Belgium

B.　　Every car was running at the finish

C.　　There were no spectators

D.　　Every car retired from the race

1962

For which of the following constructors did Dan Gurney score their only Grand Prix win?

A.　　Porsche

B.　　De Tomaso

C.　　Penske

D.　　Scarab

1963

In which Grand Prix did Jim Clark lap every other finisher?

A.   Belgian

B.   Italian

C.   Mexican

D.   Dutch

1964

At which circuit did Ferrari's Lorenzo Bandini take his sole Grand Prix victory?

A.   Zeltweg Airfield

B.   Bugatti Circuit, Le Mans

C.   Riverside

D.   Monsanto Park, Lisbon

1965

Why did Jim Clark miss the 1965 Monaco Grand Prix?

A.   He had appendicitis

B.   He was in the USA

C.   His car was damaged in a fire

D.   His passport was out of date

1966

Who scored the only Grand Prix win for a car powered by a 16-cylinder engine?

A.   Jackie Stewart

B.   Graham Hill

C.   Peter Arundell

D.   Jim Clark

1967

At which Grand Prix did the Ford Cosworth DFV engine make its debut?

A.   French

B.   Dutch

C.   Belgian

D.   British

1968

Who became the first driver to use a full-face crash helmet in a Grand Prix?

A.   Jackie Stewart

B.   Jo Bonnier

C.   Dan Gurney

D.   Jacky Ickx

1969

In a season dominated by Jackie Stewart, which other driver also led over 100 race laps?

A.   Jacky Ickx

B.   Graham Hill

C.   Denny Hulme

D.   Jochen Rindt

1970

Who won the first Grand Prix of the new decade?

A.　　Jack Brabham

B.　　Jackie Stewart

C.　　Jacky Ickx

D.　　Jochen Rindt

1971

At the Italian Grand Prix, what was the gap between the winner Peter Gethin and fifth place man Howden Ganley?

A.　　1.34 seconds

B.　　0.61 seconds

C.　　3.15 seconds

D.　　0.26 seconds

1972

Who scored BRM's final Grand Prix win?

A.　　Jean-Pierre Beltoise

B.　　Helmut Marko

C.　　Peter Gethin

D.　　Niki Lauda

1973

Jackie Stewart retired at the end of this season, having started how many Grands Prix?

A.   100

B.   102

C.   96

D.   99

1974

How many drivers notched their first Grand Prix victory in the 1974 season?

A.   Three

B.   Five

C.   One

D.   None

1975

What did Vittorio Brambilla do immediately after winning the rain-shortened Austrian Grand Prix?

A.   Continue at race speed

B.   Slide into a crash barrier

C.   Jump into the crowd

D.   Stall after stopping to collect a flag

1976

How many Grands Prix did Niki Lauda win in 1976 before his accident at the Nürburgring?

A.   Five

B.   Four

C.   Six

D.   Two

1977

In which Grand Prix did Jacques Laffite score his and Ligier's first victory in F1?

A.   Belgium

B.   Spanish

C.   Austrian

D.   Swedish

1978

Which team was sued by another team over the design of its 1978 F1 car?

A.   Martini

B.   Tyrrell

C.   Arrows

D.   Shadow

1979

The French Grand Prix featured a memorable scrap for second place. Who won the race?

A.   Alan Jones

B.   Jean-Pierre Jabouille

C.   Jody Scheckter

D.   Jacques Laffite

1980

Which Grand Prix was subsequently downgraded to a non-championship race?

A.   South Africa

B.   San Marino

C.   Spain

D.   France

1981

What team scored the first Grand Prix win for a car with a wholly carbonfibre monocoque?

A.   Williams

B.   McLaren

C.   Renault

D.   Brabham

1982

Which driver won the 1982 Brazilian Grand Prix on the road only to later be disqualified?

A.   Keke Rosberg

B.   Carlos Reutemann

C.   Nelson Piquet

D.   Niki Lauda

1983

In what position did race-winner John Watson qualify for the US (West) Grand Prix?

A.   22nd

B.   17th

C.   26th

D.   14th

1984

Which future world champion crashed when leading the 1984 Monaco Grand Prix?

A.   Ayrton Senna

B.   Nigel Mansell

C.   Alain Prost

D.   Nelson Piquet

1985

Who finished third in Australia in spite of having only three working wheels at the end of the race?

A.   Jacques Laffite

B.   Ayrton Senna

C.   Philippe Streiff

D.   Stefan Johansson

19

1986

What was unique (at the time) about the 1986 F1 season?

A.   There was no Grand Prix in Italy

B.   Only turbocharged engines were permitted

C.   There were no wet races

D.   Tyre changes were not allowed

1987

Who won the Jim Clark Trophy?

A.   Phillipe Streiff

B.   Jonathan Palmer

C.   Ivan Capelli

D.   Philippe Alliot

1988

Who collided with Senna at Monza, thus ending McLaren's chances of winning every Grand Prix that season?

A.   Jean-Louis Schlesser

B.   Piercarlo Ghinzani

C.   Bernd Schneider

D.   Oscar Larrauri

1989

Who won the Japanese Grand Prix after Senna was disqualified?

A.   Nigel Mansell

B.   Gerhard Berger

C.   Thierry Boutsen

D.   Alessandro Nannini

1990

Adrian Newey designed which of the following 1990 F1 cars?

A.   Leyton House CG901

B.   Williams FW13B

C.   McLaren MP4/5B

D.   Lotus 102

1991

Who won the 1991 Canadian Grand Prix after race-leader Nigel Mansell's Williams ground to a halt on the last lap?

A.   Riccardo Patrese

B.   Ayrton Senna

C.   Nelson Piquet

D.   Gerhard Berger

1992

For which team did Damon Hill make his Grand Prix debut?

A.   Brabham

B.   Williams

C.   Lotus

D.   Tyrrell

1993

Who did Mika Hakkinen replace as Ayrton Senna's team-mate at McLaren?

A.   Michael Andretti

B.   Johnny Herbert

C.   Karl Wendlinger

D.   Mark Blundell

1994

Which of the following drivers was NOT suspended from at least one Grand Prix during the 1994 season?

A.   Eddie Irvine

B.   Jean Alesi

C.   Michael Schumacher

D.   Mika Hakkinen

1995

With which team did Nigel Mansell end his career as an F1 driver?

A.   Ferrari

B.   Williams

C.   Jordan

D.   McLaren

1996

Whose crash helmet did David Coulthard wear in the Monaco Grand Prix?

A.   Mika Hakkinen

B.   Michael Schumacher

C.   Martin Brundle

D.   Rubens Barrichello

1997

In which 1997 Grand Prix did the top three in qualifying all set the same time to a thousandth of a second?

A.   Portuguese

B.   Luxembourg (Nurburgring)

C.   Austrian

D.   European (Jerez)

1998

In which 1998 Grand Prix did Michael Schumacher take the chequered flag (and the win) in the pit lane?

A.   Austrian

B.   Belgian

C.   British

D.   Hungarian

24

1999

Who won the last Grand Prix of the millennium?

A.   Mika Hakkinen

B.   Michael Schumacher

C.   David Coulthard

D.   Heinz-Harald Frentzen

2000

What was different about the 2000 British Grand Prix?

A.   The Safety Car led the most laps

B.   It took place in April rather than July

C.   It was run anti-clockwise

D.   It was a non-championship race

2001

For which team did Jean Alesi drive the last five Grands Prix of his F1 career?

A.   Jordan

B.   Sauber

C.   Prost

D.   Arrows

2002

Which British driver raced for Toyota in their debut season in Formula One in 2002?

A.   Johnny Herbert

B.   Allan McNish

C.   Oliver Gavin

D.   Anthony Davidson

2003

Who became the youngest-ever Grand Prix winner (at the time) during the 2003 F1 season?

A.   Kimi Raikkonen

B.   Jenson Button

C.   Felipe Massa

D.   Fernando Alonso

2004

How many Grands Prix (out of eighteen contested) did Ferrari win in 2004?

A.   Fifteen

B.   Eighteen

C.   Twelve

D.   Sixteen

2005

Who took Ralf Schumacher's place in qualifying for the United States Grand Prix?

A.   Pedro de la Rosa

B.   Robert Doornbos

C.   Ricardo Zonta

D.   Scott Speed

2006

Where did Michael Schumacher finish in Brazil, his last Grand Prix for Ferrari?

A.   First

B.   Third

C.   Sixth

D.   Fourth

2007

With two Grands Prix left, by how many points did Kimi Raikkonen trail Lewis Hamilton in the championship standings?

A.   Seventeen

B.   Eighteen

C.   Fourteen

D.   Fifteen

2008

On which lap of the Singapore Grand Prix did Nelson Piquet Jr. infamously crash out of the race?

A.   Ten

B.   Fourteen

C.   Seventeen

D.   Nineteen

2009

Who partnered Kimi Raikkonen at Ferrari for the last five Grands Prix of the season?

A.   Giancarlo Fisichella

B.   Luciano Burti

C.   Vitantonio Liuzzi

D.   Luca Badoer

2010

Red Bull team-mates Vettel and Webber collided when disputing the lead of which Grand Prix?

A.   Korea

B.   Turkey

C.   Singapore

D.   Malaysia

2011

Who finished second to Sebastian Vettel in the Drivers' Championship?

A.   Fernando Alonso

B.   Lewis Hamilton

C.   Mark Webber

D.   Jenson Button

2012

In which Grand Prix did Michael Schumacher score his 155th and last podium finish?

A.   Bahrain

B.   Belgium

C.   India

D.   Europe (Valencia)

2013

For which team did Charles Pic drive in 2013?

A.   Caterham

B.   Marussia

C.   HRT

D.   Virgin

2014

In what place did Sebastian Vettel finish in the 2014 world championship?

A.   Second

B.   Fifth

C.   Fourth

D.   Third

2015

Where did McLaren finish in the 2015 Constructors' standings?

A.   Fifth

B.   Tenth

C.   Seventh

D.   Ninth

2016

Who replaced Rio Haryanto at Manor from the Belgian Grand Prix onwards?

A. Esteban Ocon

B. Stoffel Vandoorne

C. Sergey Sirotkin

D. Pascal Wehrlein

2017

Which driver won the 'Breakthrough of the year' award (for achievements in 2016) at the Laureus Sports Awards?

A. Esteban Ocon

B. Max Verstappen

C. Nico Rosberg

D. Carlos Sainz, Jr.

2018

In which race was the chequered flag mistakenly shown a lap too soon?

A. Azerbaijan

B. Germany

C. Canada

D. Mexico

2019

At which Grand Prix did Charles Leclerc take his first pole position in Formula One?

A.   Austria

B.   Bahrain

C.   China

D.   Spain

2020

What does the acronym DAS stand for on the Mercedes W11?

A.   Damper Adjustment System

B.   Dual Axis Steering

C.   Dynamic Antistall Software

D.   Directional Aero System

General Knowledge I

G1

Which country has hosted the most Grands Prix?

A.   Great Britain

B.   France

C.   Italy

D.   Germany

G2

Who did Michael Schumacher replace at Jordan when he made his F1 debut?

A.   Andrea de Cesaris

B.   Roberto Moreno

C.   Mauricio Gugelmin

D.   Bertrand Gachot

G3

In what year did the six-wheel Tyrrell P34 make its debut?

A.   1978

B.   1976

C.   1974

D.   1977

G4

Who is the only driver to have won the world championship with both Ferrari and McLaren?

A.   Kimi Raikkonen

B.   Niki Lauda

C.   Alain Prost

D.   Ayrton Senna

G5

Who replaced Alain Prost at Ferrari for the final Grand Prix in 1991?

A.   Ivan Capelli

B.   Nicola Larini

C.   Emanuele Pirro

D.   Gianni Morbidelli

G6

What team won Grands Prix in 1982 with two different engines?

A.   Brabham

B.   Lotus

C.   Williams

D.   McLaren

G7

In what season did a stray priest result in a Safety Car at the British Grand Prix?

A.   2003

B.   2005

C.   2000

D.   2008

G8

How many drivers have retired immediately from F1 after winning the world championship?

A.   Two

B.   Four

C.   Six

D.   One

G9

Where did Michael Schumacher notch his first Grand Prix victory?

A.   Hungaroring

B.   Spa-Francorchamps

C.   Estoril

D.   Imola

G10

How many drivers have won both the F1 world championship and the Indy 500?

A.   Two

B.   Five

C.   One

D.   Three

General Knowledge II

G11

How many Grands Prix were won by cars powered by BRM's V12 engine?

A.   One

B.   Four

C.   Six

D.   Two

G12

What was Swedish driver Tommy 'Slim' Borgudd's other job?

A.   Model

B.   Pilot in the Swedish Air Force

C.   Session drummer who had worked with Abba

D.   Master brewer for Carlsberg

G13

For which team did 1976 world champion James Hunt last race in F1?

A.   McLaren

B.   Fittipaldi

C.   Brabham

D.   Wolf

G14

What was the type number of the Lotus F1 car that made its debut in 1969?

A.   Type 56

B.   Type 63

C.   Type 70

D.   Type 72

G15

Which driver holds the record for the longest time between Grand Prix wins?

A.   Rubens Barrichello

B.   Riccardo Patrese

C.   Kimi Raikkonen

D.   John Watson

G16

Who has won all three Indian Grands Prix to date?

A.   Sebastian Vettel

B.   Fernando Alonso

C.   Lewis Hamilton

D.   Nico Rosberg

G17

For which team did Damon Hill drive in 1997?

A.   Williams

B.   Prost

C.   Jordan

D.   Arrows

G18

Which is the only circuit on the F1 calendar to use a figure of 8 layout?

A.   Monza

B.   Singapore

C.   Circuit of the Americas

D.   Suzuka

G19

Who was the only driver to race in F1 for both Matra teams?

A.   Johnny Servoz-Gavin

B.   Jean-Pierre Beltoise

C.   Jackie Stewart

D.   Henri Pescarolo

G20

Chris Amon drove for how many different constructors in F1?

A.   Thirteen

B.   Ten

C.   Fifteen

D.   Eight

General Knowledge III

G21

Which of the following British drivers did NOT drive for Team Lotus in a Grand Prix?

A.   Jim Crawford

B.   Tony Trimmer

C.   John Watson

D.   Brian Henton

G22

Who is the last defending F1 world champion not to have won a Grand Prix in the season following his title win?

A.   Jacques Villeneuve

B.   Damon Hill

C.   Michael Schumacher

D.   Sebastian Vettel

G23

Who was the youngest driver to race in a Grand Prix in 2019?

A.   Pierre Gasly

B.   Lando Norris

C.   George Russell

D.   Lance Stroll

G24

What career did Jaime Alguersuari pursue after retiring from motorsport at the age of 25?

A.   Jockey

B.   Model

C.   Disc jockey

D.   Stuntman

G25

Who raced for Ferrari in the 1952 Indianapolis 500?

A.   Nino Farina

B.   Alberto Ascari

C.   Piero Taruffi

D.   Rudi Fischer

G26

How many Grands Prix did Lewis Hamilton win at McLaren?

A.   Twenty-four

B.   Eighteen

C.   Sixteen

D.   Twenty-one

G27

By what other surname was Ayrton Senna known?

A.   da Silva

B.   Dos Santos

C.   Caixinha

D.   Soutomaior

G28

Which driver scored the last Grand Prix win for a front-engined car?

A.   Ronnie Bucknum

B.   Dan Gurney

C.   Richie Ginther

D.   Phil Hill

G29

Which of the following drivers has NOT raced for Sauber in a Grand Prix?

A.   Felipe Nasr

B.   Adrian Sutil

C.   Sergey Sirotkin

D.   Antonio Giovinazzi

G30

For which team did Niki Lauda first race in F1?

A.   March

B.   Surtees

C.   Eiffelland

D.   Brabham

General Knowledge IV

G31

How many children of F1 world champions have won the world championship?

A.   One

B.   Two

C.   Four

D.   None

G32

For which of these teams did Mario Andretti NOT drive in F1?

A.   March

B.   Ferrari

C.   Brabham

D.   Williams

G33

Apart from Nino Farina, who is the only driver to have won a Grand Prix at the first attempt?

A.   Juan Manuel Fangio

B.   Lorenzo Bandini

C.   Jacques Villeneuve

D.   Giancarlo Baghetti

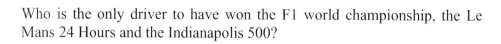

G34

Who is the only driver to have won the F1 world championship, the Le Mans 24 Hours and the Indianapolis 500?

A.   Jochen Rindt

B.   Graham Hill

C.   Jim Clark

D.   Emerson Fittipaldi

G35

Who was the first Swiss driver to win a Grand Prix?

A.   Romain Grosjean

B.   Clay Regazzoni

C.   Jo Siffert

D.   Marc Surer

G36

For which of the following teams did Jos Verstappen NOT race in F1?

A.   Jordan

B.   Simtek

C.   Minardi

D.   Stewart

G37

"Mineral Water" is the English translation of the name of a corner at which circuit?

A.   Spa-Francorchamps

B.   Imola

C.   Paul Ricard

D.   Magny Cours

G38

With whom does Lewis Hamilton share the record for the most Grand Prix wins in a debut season?

A.   Juan Manuel Fangio

B.   Jacques Villeneuve

C.   Nino Farina

D.   Damon Hill

G39

Why was Patrick Depailler's 1979 season cut short?

A.   He had a hang-gliding accident

B.   He was called up by the French military

C.   He fell off the roof of his house

D.   He went on a pilgrimage

G40

How many Brazilian drivers have won a Grand Prix?

A.   Nine

B.   Three

C.   Twelve

D.   Six

General Knowledge V

G41

For which team did Sebastian Vettel make his Grand Prix debut?

A.   Toro Rosso

B.   BMW Sauber

C.   Red Bull Racing

D.   Renault

G42

Which car won the most Grands Prix in a single season?

A.   McLaren MP4-4

B.   Ferrari F2004

C.   Mercedes W07

D.   Ferrari F2002

G43

Who is the only driver to have scored multiple Grand Prix wins but no other podium finishes?

A.   Maurice Trintignant

B.   Peter Revson

C.   Jean-Pierre Jabouille

D.   Pedro Rodriguez

G44

Who replaced Niki Lauda at Brabham during the 1979 season?

A.   Francois Hesnault

B.   Hector Rebaque

C.   Gianfranco Brancatelli

D.   Ricardo Zunino

G45

What is the smallest ever margin of victory in the World Drivers' Championship?

A.   1 point

B.   0.5 points

C.   2 points

D.   0 points – the championship was decided on countback

G46

How many drivers have won the world championship?

A.   33

B.   29

C.   37

D.   42

G47

How many times has the world championship been won by a driver who scored only one race victory that season?

A.   Once

B.   Twice

C.   Never

D.   Three times

G48

Former Brabham designer Gordon Murray also designed which supercar?

A.   Pagani Zonda

B.   McLaren F1

C.   Aston Martin Vanquish

D.   Ferrari Enzo

G49

Who is the only driver to have led a Grand Prix in a Minardi?

A.   Fernando Alonso

B.   Alessandro Nannini

C.   Michele Alboreto

D.   Pierluigi Martini

G50

In how many seasons has the same driver won both the first and last Grands Prix?

A.   12

B.   20

C.   26

D.   17

General Knowledge VI

G51

What is Nico Hulkenberg's best race finish in F1?

A. Fourth

B. Third

C. Sixth

D. Fifth

G52

For which team did Paul di Resta make a one-off appearance in 2017?

A. Sauber

B. Force India

C. Renault

D. Williams

G53

Which of these drivers contested the most Grands Prix for Toro Rosso?

A. Scott Speed

B. Sébastien Buemi

C. Jaime Alguersuari

D. Sebastien Bourdais

G54

Who set the first sub-7 minute lap of the Nürburgring Nordschleife in an F1 car?

A. Niki Lauda

B. James Hunt

C. Jody Scheckter

D. Ronnie Peterson

G55

Which of these drivers won their first Grand Prix in the fewest attempts?

A. Sebastian Vettel

B. Jacques Villeneuve

C. Fernando Alonso

D. Lewis Hamilton

G56

Who took the only pole position for the Toleman F1 team?

A. Johnny Cecotto

B. Teo Fabi

C. Ayrton Senna

D. Derek Warwick

G57

Which of the following Grands Prix did Michael Schumacher never win?

A. Bahrain

B. Portugal

C. China

D. Turkey

G58

For which team did Jonathan Palmer make his F1 debut?

A. Zakspeed

B. Tyrrell

C. Williams

D. RAM

G59

Who among these drivers took the most pole positions in F1?

A. Nelson Piquet

B. Fernando Alonso

C. Nigel Mansell

D. Alain Prost

G60

Which French circuit featured a cobbled hairpin?

A.   Rouen-les-Essarts

B.   Charade (Clermont-Ferrand)

C.   Reims-Gueux

D.   Dijon-Prenois

General Knowledge VII

G61

Who was the first driver to start 200 Grands Prix?

A.   Riccardo Patrese

B.   Jarno Trulli

C.   Rubens Barrichello

D.   Michael Schumacher

G62

At which of these circuits was the 1950 Grand Prix won at the highest average speed?

A.   Silverstone

B.   Monza

C.   Spa-Francorchamps

D.   Reims-Gueux

G63

Who scored the last Grand Prix victory for a 12-cylinder engine?

A.   Ayrton Senna

B.   Gerhard Berger

C.   Jean Alesi

D.   Alain Prost

G64

In what year was the South African Grand Prix last run?

A.   1978

B.   1993

C.   1985

D.   1991

G65

Who scored Honda's first Grand Prix victory?

A.   John Surtees

B.   Dan Gurney

C.   Ronnie Bucknum

D.   Richie Ginther

G66

In which year did British drivers finish first, second, third, fourth and fifth-equal in the world championship?

A.   1958

B.   1962

C.   1964

D.   1965

G67

Who did Nick Heidfeld replace at BMW Sauber during the 2010 season?

A.   Robert Kubica

B.   Pedro de la Rosa

C.   Jacques Villeneuve

D.   Adrian Sutil

G68

Who was the first driver to win a Grand Prix in three different decades?

A.   Jack Brabham

B.   Graham Hill

C.   Dan Gurney

D.   Michael Schumacher

G69

In which year did the Australian Grand Prix start the season, four months after bringing the previous season to a close?

A.   1999

B.   1996

C.   2000

D.   1991

G70

Who is the oldest driver to have raced in a Grand Prix?

A.   Maurice Trintignant

B.   Luigi Fagioli

C.   Juan Manuel Fangio

D.   Louis Chiron

The Drivers I

D1

Who is the only driver to have led every Grand Prix in which he raced?

A.   Alberto Ascari

B.   Nicola Larini

C.   Juan Manuel Fangio

D.   Markus Winkelhock

D2

By what title is former Lotus driver Johnny Dumfries also known?

A.   The Duke of Roxburghe

B.   The Marquess of Bute

C.   The Earl of Wemyss and March

D.   The Duke of Hamilton

D3

For which team did Jarno Trulli take his only Grand Prix victory?

A.   Renault

B.   Toyota

C.   Prost

D.   Jordan

D4

How many Scottish drivers have won a Grand Prix?

A.   Three

B.   Four

C.   Five

D.   Two

D5

Tyrrell star Francois Cevert's brother-in-law was also an F1 driver. Who was he?

A.   Patrick Depailler

B.   Henri Pescarolo

C.   Jo Siffert

D.   Jean-Pierre Beltoise

D6

Who did Sebastian Vettel depose as the youngest driver to win the world championship?

A.   Fernando Alonso

B.   Emerson Fittipaldi

C.   Lewis Hamilton

D.   Michael Schumacher

D7

Which 1970s Grand Prix driver was known as 'the Monza Gorilla'?

A.   Renzo Zorzi

B.   Clay Regazzoni

C.   Vittorio Brambilla

D.   Arturo Merzario

D8

In what year did Nigel Mansell make his F1 debut?

A.   1980

B.   1979

C.   1982

D.   1984

D9

How many times did Michael and Ralf Schumacher finish first and second in a Grand Prix?

A.   Nine

B.   Seven

C.   Five

D.   Three

D10

How many points did 1979 world champion Jody Scheckter score in 1980?

A. Two

B. None

C. Three

D. Four

The Drivers II

D11

Who was the first woman to race in a Grand Prix?

A.   Lella Lombardi

B.   Maria Teresa de Filippis

C.   Desiré Wilson

D.   Davina Galica

D12

Mike Hawthorn and which other world champion each won 3 Grands Prix in their career?

A.   Nino Farina

B.   Keke Rosberg

C.   Denny Hulme

D.   Phil Hill

D13

How many Grands Prix did Niki Lauda win at McLaren?

A.   Six

B.   Ten

C.   Twelve

D.   Eight

D14

In which year did Denny Hulme win the World Drivers' Championship?

A.   1967

B.   1964

C.   1966

D.   1970

D15

In 1973, the George Medal was awarded to which two British F1 drivers?

A.   James Hunt and Jackie Stewart

B.   Mike Hailwood and David Purley

C.   Graham Hill and Jackie Oliver

D.   Mike Beuttler and John Watson

D16

Who is the only one of the following drivers to have driven for Williams in the season after winning the world championship with them?

A.   Nigel Mansell

B.   Damon Hill

C.   Jacques Villeneuve

D.   Nelson Piquet

D17

How many times was Stirling Moss runner-up in the world championship?

A. Three

B. Four

C. Six

D. Two

D18

In what year did David Coulthard's spin trigger a first lap pile-up at Spa?

A. 1998

B. 1999

C. 2000

D. 2001

D19

How many Grands Prix did Eddie Irvine win at Ferrari?

A. Four

B. Two

C. Seven

D. Six

D20

Who was the last Italian driver to win a Grand Prix for Ferrari?

A.   Jean Alesi

B.   Michele Alboreto

C.   Clay Regazzoni

D.   Ivan Capelli

The Teams I

T1

In which year did Honda's 'Earth car' livery appear?

A.   2007

B.   2008

C.   2004

D.   2009

T2

Eddie Jordan sold his F1 team in 2005. Under which name did the team start the 2006 season?

A.   Marussia

B.   HRT

C.   Spyker

D.   Midland

T3

Which of these F1 teams used their own W12 engine?

A.   Andrea Moda

B.   Life

C.   Kauhsen

D.   Maki

T4

What engines did Williams use during the 1988 season?

A.   Judd

B.   Honda

C.   Hart

D.   Renault

T5

Which team was purchased by Benetton in 1985?

A.   Arrows

B.   Osella

C.   Toleman

D.   Zakspeed

T6

Which F1 team was owned by Bernie Ecclestone?

A.   March

B.   Brabham

C.   Shadow

D.   Arrows

T7

Which of these world champions did NOT race for his own F1 team?

A.   Graham Hill

B.   Jackie Stewart

C.   John Surtees

D.   Emerson Fittipaldi

T8

Which team was the first to win fifty Grands Prix?

A.   Ferrari

B.   Maserati

C.   Lotus

D.   Cooper

T9

Who scored the first Grand Prix victory for Williams?

A.   Clay Regazzoni

B.   Carlos Reutemann

C.   Alan Jones

D.   Keke Rosberg

T10

Which was the only team to race a gas turbine-powered car in F1?

A.   Matra

B.   Ferrari

C.   McLaren

D.   Lotus

The Teams II

T11

In which year did Williams last win a Grand Prix?

A.   2012

B.   2008

C.   2014

D.   2005

T12

Which of the following F1 Team Principals also raced in a Grand Prix?

A.   Gerrard Larrousse

B.   Bernie Ecclestone

C.   Christian Horner

D.   Colin Chapman

T13

Who won the first Grand Prix for McLaren as a constructor?

A.   Denny Hulme

B.   Dan Gurney

C.   Bruce McLaren

D.   Peter Revson

T14

Which F1 engine did McLaren test, but not use in a Grand Prix, in 1993?

A.   Lamborghini

B.   Renault

C.   Peugeot

D.   Yamaha

T15

Who succeeded Stefano Domenicali as the Team Principal of Scuderia Ferrari?

A.   Mauricio Arrivabene

B.   Marco Mattiacci

C.   Mattia Binotto

D.   Sante Ghedini

T16

For which team did Ron Dennis first work in F1?

A.   McLaren

B.   BRM

C.   Brabham

D.   Cooper

T17

The ATS team that competed in F1 from 1977 to 1984 shared its acronym with a previous F1 team from which country?

A. Italy

B. France

C. Spain

D. United Kingdom

T18

In which decade did Scuderia Ferrari win the most Grands Prix?

A. 1950s

B. 1970s

C. 1990s

D. 2000s

T19

Which Grand Prix-winning team beseeched The Great Chicken in the Sky to supply a replacement engine?

A. March

B. Hesketh

C. Shadow

D. Tyrrell

T20

Which constructor won every Grand Prix in 1950?

A.   ERA

B.   Ferrari

C.   Alfa Romeo

D.   Talbot Lago

Surely Not I

S1

Why did David Coulthard retire from the 1995 Australian GP?

A.   He crashed at the pit lane entrance

B.   He spun on the formation lap

C.   His fire extinguisher exploded

D.   He hit the Safety Car

S2

Who protested about the early start of the warm-up session for the 1984 Dallas Grand Prix by turning up in his pyjamas?

A.   Nelson Piquet

B.   Jacques Laffite

C.   Ayrton Senna

D.   Keke Rosberg

S3

By what means did Harry Schell qualify 3rd for the 1959 United States Grand Prix?

A.   His car was 100 kg underweight

B.   He took a shortcut

C.   The timekeeepers made an error

D.   The grid positions were drawn by lots

S4

Which F1 driver was kidnapped in Cuba in 1958?

A.   Stirling Moss

B.   Juan Manuel Fangio

C.   Wolfgang von Trips

D.   Olivier Gendebien

S5

Apart from Alberto Ascari, which other driver has crashed into the harbour during the Monaco Grand Prix?

A.   Maurice Trintignant

B.   Johnny Servoz-Gavin

C.   Paul Hawkins

D.   Frank Gardner

S6

Who crashed heavily in the 2003 Brazilian GP yet finished third?

A.   Rubens Barrichello

B.   Juan Pablo Montoya

C.   Fernando Alonso

D.   Mark Webber

S7

What happened to Taki Inoue at the 1995 Hungarian Grand Prix?

A.   His crash helmet visor seized open

B.   He was run over by a course car

C.   His drinks bottle exploded

D.   His rear wing fell off on the grid

S8

Who punched a marshal after crashing out of the 1977 Canadian Grand Prix?

A.   James Hunt

B.   Carlos Reutemann

C.   Jody Scheckter

D.   Vittorio Brambilla

S9

What caused Gerhard Berger to retire from the 1995 Italian Grand Prix?

A.   His left front wheel fell off

B.   His suspension was broken by a stray camera

C.   His engine cover exploded

D.   His car was hit by a loose advertising board

S10

Who failed to qualify for, retired, and was disqualified from the same race?

A.   Alex Dias Ribeiro

B.   Hans Heyer

C.   Arturo Merzario

D.   Danny Ongais

Surely Not II

S11

Who declined to write the foreword for the Autocourse annual?

A.   Ayrton Senna

B.   Jody Scheckter

C.   Michael Schumacher

D.   Fernando Alonso

S12

Why was Adrian Newey 'asked to leave' Repton School?

A.   He blew up the toilets

B.   He drove a Mini into the swimming pool

C.   He damaged centuries-old stained glass windows

D.   He put laxatives in the soup

S13

Why was F1 team owner Rob Walker banned from flying in the 1930s?

A.   He used a plane to jump the fences on a racecourse

B.   He flew under Tower Bridge

C.   He flew through a hangar

D.   He was caught using a stretch of the A4 as a runway

S14

Who lapped Watkins Glen 9.5 seconds faster than anyone in a wet practice session in 1979?

A.   Alan Jones

B.   Nelson Piquet

C.   Gilles Villeneuve

D.   Carlos Reutemann

S15

In which year did the drivers who finished first and second in the world championship never both finish a race in podium positions?

A.   1971

B.   1950

C.   1998

D.   1983

S16

At which circuit could 'The Bog', an area infamous for spectator misbehaviour, be found?

A.   Interlagos

B.   Kyalami

C.   Brand's Hatch

D.   Watkins Glen

S17

Which of these drivers missed a Grand Prix, having been suspended by his team?

A.   James Hunt

B.   Ayrton Senna

C.   Fernando Alonso

D.   Kimi Raikkonen

S18

What did Nelson Piquet do after retiring from the 1982 German Grand Prix?

A.   Join spectators for a beer

B.   Assault the driver with whom he had collided

C.   Rejoin the race in his spare car

D.   Hit his car with a tree branch

S19

In which 1967 Grand Prix did Jim Clark re-take the race lead after losing a lap due to a puncture?

A.   Italy

B.   Britain

C.   United States

D.   Dutch

Which driver took part in a powerboat race wearing a gorilla suit?

A.   James Hunt

B.   Kimi Raikkonen

C.   Gerhard Berger

D.   Daniel Ricciardo

Defunct Constructors

List the following constructors, none of whom now compete in F1 *as constructors*, in descending order according to their number of Grand Prix victories.

Benetton

Brabham

Brawn

BRM

Cooper

Honda

Jordan

Ligier

Lotus F1 (2012 To 2015)

March

Maserati

Matra

Team Lotus (1958 To 1994)

Vanwall

Wolf

Tyrrell

1950s Grand Prix Winners

Fourteen drivers each won one or more Grands Prix in the 1950s. How many of them can you name?

To help you a little, I have listed the nationality of each driver and their respective number of wins, including shared wins, in that decade.

24 wins	Argentinian
13 wins	Italian
12 wins	English
6 wins	English
5 wins	Italian
3 wins	English
3 wins	English
2 wins	Argentinian
2 wins	Australian
2 wins	French
1 win	Italian
1 win	Italian
1 win	Italian
1 win	Swedish

Most Wins For Scuderia Ferrari

As at the end of the 2019 season, thirteen drivers have each won five or more Grands Prix for Scuderia Ferrari. Can you name them all?

To help a little, I've listed their nationalities and the number of Grands Prix they won for Ferrari.

72 wins	German
15 wins	Austrian
14 wins	German
13 wins	Italian
11 wins	Brazilian
11 wins	Spanish
10 wins	Finnish
9 wins	Brazilian
6 wins	Canadian
6 wins	Belgian
5 wins	French
5 wins	Austrian
5 wins	Argentinian

The Long And The Short

Arrange the following circuits from the 2019 F1 season in *descending* order according to their lap length – i.e begin with the longest and end with the shortest.

Circuit Of The Americas

Hungaroring

Marina Bay Street Circuit

Monaco

Monza

Paul Ricard

Red Bull Ring

Spa-Francorchamps

Silverstone

Suzuka

Most Starts Without A Win

Name the ten drivers to have started the most Grands Prix, without having won at least one of them as at the end of the 2019 season.

To help you a little, I have listed the number of race starts and nationality of each driver.

208 starts   Italian

183 starts   German

177 starts   German

176 starts   Mexican

166 starts   French

165 starts   English

162 starts   English

143 starts   French

143 starts   American (USA)

128 starts   German

First Grands Prix: Countries

Starting with the earliest, list the following countries in the order in which they first held a grand prix.

Argentina

Austria

Bahrain

Brazil

Canada

Hungary

India

Japan

Malaysia

Mexico

Russia

Singapore

Spain

Switzerland

USA

Most Turbo Wins: 1979-1988

Name the fifteen drivers who each won at least one Grand Prix in a turbocharged F1 car between 1979 and 1988.

To aid you, I've listed the number of turbo-powered wins and the nationality of each driver.

35 wins	French
14 wins	Brazilian
14 wins	Brazilian
13 wins	English
7 wins	French
6 wins	Austrian
4 wins	Austrian
3 wins	Finnish
3 wins	Italian
2 wins	French
2 wins	Canadian
2 wins	French
2 wins	French
1 win	Italian
1 win	Italian

Champions With More Than One Team

Name the ten drivers who, as at the end of the 2019 season, have won the World Drivers' Championship with more than one team.

To help out a bit, I've listed the number of different teams with which they won championships and the decade(s) in which they did so.

Four teams   1950s

Two teams   1950s and 1960s

Two teams   1960s

Two teams   1960s and 1970s

Two teams   1970s

Two teams   1970s and 1980s

Two teams   1980s

Two teams   1980s and 1990s

Two teams   1990s and 2000s

Two teams   2000s and 2010s

1982 Grand Prix Winners

Name the eleven drivers who each won one or more Grands Prix in 1982. To help you, I've listed the teams they drove for and the number of Grands Prix they won.

Ferrari	2 wins
McLaren	2 wins
McLaren	2 wins
Renault	2 wins
Renault	2 wins
Brabham	1 win
Brabham	1 win
Ferrari	1 win
Lotus	1 win
Tyrrell	1 win
Williams	1 win

Podiums By US Drivers

As at the end of 2019, eleven drivers from the USA have finished on the podium in at least one Grand Prix. Name as many of them as you can.

To help you a bit, I've listed both the number of podium finishes attained by each driver and the period during which he raced in F1 (albeit not necessarily continuously).

19 podiums   1968-1982

19 podiums   1959-1970

16 podiums   1958-1966

14 podiums   1960-1967

9 podiums   1978-1989

8 podiums   1964-1974

3 podiums   1957-1965

2 podiums   1950-1960

1 podium   1971-1975

1 podium   1973

1 podium   1993

Sub-Ten Podium Club: 2010-19

Twelve drivers scored between one and nine podium finishes between the start of the 2010 season and the end of the 2019 season. Can you name them all?

To assist you a little, I've listed the number of podiums and nationality of each driver

8 podiums	Mexican
3 podiums	Polish
3 podiums	Russian
1 podium	Russian
1 podium	Japanese
1 podium	German
1 podium	Spanish
1 podium	French
1 podium	Canadian
1 podium	Danish
1 podium	Venezuelan
1 podium	German

The Runners-Up

As of the end of the 2019 season, nineteen drivers have a career-best finish of second place in the Drivers World Championship.

Your task is to name them. To help you, I've listed the year(s) in which they finished runner-up in the standings.

1954

1955/56/57/58

1959

1960

1961

1969, 1970

1974

1971, 1978

1979

1981

1982

1985

1992

1997

1999

2001

2002, 2004

2008

2019

Part Two: The Answers

1950 to 1959

1950	B.	Silverstone
1951	B.	None
1952	C.	Juan Manuel Fangio
1953	D.	Argentinian
1954	C.	Maserati
1955	A.	Aintree
1956	B.	He handed over his car to Fangio
1957	C.	Pescara, Italy
1958	C.	Mike Hawthorn
1959	D.	Jo Bonnier

1960 to 1969

1960	C.	Stirling Moss
1961	B.	Every car was running at the finish
1962	A.	Porsche
1963	D.	Dutch
1964	A.	Zeltweg Airfield
1965	B.	He was in the USA
1966	D.	Jim Clark
1967	B.	Dutch
1968	C.	Dan Gurney
1969	D.	Jochen Rindt

1970 to 1979

1970	A.	Jack Brabham
1971	B.	0.61 seconds
1972	A.	Jean-Pierre Beltoise
1973	D.	99
1974	A.	Three
1975	B.	Slide into a crash barrier
1976	A.	Five
1977	D.	Swedish
1978	C.	Arrows
1979	B.	Jean-Pierre Jabouille

1980 to 1989

1980   C.   Spain

1981   B.   McLaren

1982   C.   Nelson Piquet

1983   A.   22nd

1984   B.   Nigel Mansell

1985   C.   Philippe Streiff

1986   B.   Only turbocharged engines were permitted

1987   B.   Jonathan Palmer

1988   A.   Jean-Louis Schlesser

1989   D.   Alessandro Nannini

1990 to 1999

1990	A.	Leyton House CG901
1991	C.	Nelson Piquet
1992	A.	Brabham
1993	A.	Michael Andretti
1994	B.	Jean Alesi
1995	D.	McLaren
1996	B.	Michael Schumacher
1997	D.	European (Jerez)
1998	C.	British
1999	A.	Mika Hakkinen

2000 to 2009

2000	B.	It took place in April rather than July
2001	A.	Jordan
2002	B.	Allan McNish
2003	D.	Fernando Alonso
2004	A.	Fifteen
2005	C.	Ricardo Zonta
2006	D.	Fourth
2007	A.	Seventeen
2008	B.	Fourteen
2009	A.	Giancarlo Fisichella

2010 to 2020

2010	B.	Turkey
2011	D.	Jenson Button
2012	D.	Europe (Valencia)
2013	A.	Caterham
2014	B.	Fifth
2015	D.	Ninth
2016	A.	Esteban Ocon
2017	C.	Nico Rosberg
2018	C.	Canada
2019	B.	Bahrain

General Knowledge I

G1   C.   Italy

G2   D.   Bertrand Gachot

G3   B.   1976

G4   B.   Niki Lauda

G5   D.   Gianni Morbidelli

G6   A.   Brabham

G7   A.   2003

G8   B.   Four

G9   B.   Spa-Francorchamps

G10   B.   Five

General Knowledge II

G11	B.	Four
G12	C.	Session drummer who had worked with Abba
G13	D.	Wolf
G14	B.	Type 63
G15	B.	Riccardo Patrese
G16	A.	Sebastian Vettel
G17	D.	Arrows
G18	D.	Suzuka
G19	B.	Jean-Pierre Beltoise
G20	A.	Thirteen

General Knowledge III

G21	B.	Tony Trimmer
G22	D.	Sebastian Vettel
G23	B.	Lando Norris
G24	C.	Disc jockey
G25	B.	Alberto Ascari
G26	D.	Twenty-one
G27	A.	da Silva
G28	D.	Phil Hill
G29	C.	Sergey Sirotkin
G30	A.	March

General Knowledge IV

G31	B.	Two
G32	C.	Brabham
G33	D.	Giancarlo Baghetti
G34	B.	Graham Hill
G35	C.	Jo Siffert
G36	A.	Jordan
G37	B.	Imola
G38	B.	Jacques Villeneuve
G39	A.	He had a hang-gliding accident
G40	D.	Six

General Knowledge V

G41	B.	BMW Sauber
G42	C.	Mercedes W07
G43	C.	Jean-Pierre Jabouille
G44	D.	Ricardo Zunino
G45	B.	0.5 points
G46	A.	33
G47	B.	Twice
G48	B.	McLaren F1
G49	D.	Pierluigi Martini
G50	B.	20

General Knowledge VI

G51	A.	Fourth
G52	D.	Williams
G53	B.	Sébastien Buemi
G54	A.	Niki Lauda
G55	B.	Jacques Villeneuve
G56	B.	Teo Fabi
G57	D.	Turkey
G58	C.	Williams
G59	D.	Alain Prost
G60	A.	Rouen-les-Essarts

General Knowledge VII

G61	A.	Riccardo Patrese
G62	C.	Spa-Francorchamps
G63	C.	Jean Alesi
G64	B.	1993
G65	D.	Richie Ginther
G66	A.	1958
G67	B.	Pedro de la Rosa
G68	A.	Jack Brabham
G69	B.	1996
G70	D.	Louis Chiron

The Drivers I

D1	D.	Markus Winkelhock
D2	B.	The Marquess of Bute
D3	A.	Renault
D4	B.	Four
D5	D.	Jean-Pierre Beltoise
D6	C.	Lewis Hamilton
D7	C.	Vittorio Brambilla
D8	A.	1980
D9	C.	Five
D10	A.	Two

The Drivers II

D11	B.	Maria Teresa de Filippis
D12	D.	Phil Hill
D13	D.	Eight
D14	A.	1967
D15	B.	Mike Hailwood and David Purley
D16	C.	Jacques Villeneuve
D17	B.	Four
D18	A.	1998
D19	A.	Four
D20	B.	Michele Alboreto

The Teams I

T1	A.	2007
T2	D.	Midland
T3	B.	Life
T4	A.	Judd
T5	C.	Toleman
T6	B.	Brabham
T7	B.	Jackie Stewart
T8	C.	Lotus
T9	A.	Clay Regazzoni
T10	D.	Lotus

The Teams II

T11	A.	2012
T12	A.	Gerrard Larrousse
T13	C.	Bruce McLaren
T14	A.	Lamborghini
T15	B.	Marco Mattiaci
T16	D.	Cooper
T17	A.	Italy
T18	D.	2000s
T19	B.	Hesketh
T20	C.	Alfa Romeo

Surely Not I

S1	A.	He crashed at the pit lane entrance
S2	B.	Jacques Laffite
S3	B.	He took a shortcut
S4	B.	Juan Manuel Fangio
S5	C.	Paul Hawkins
S6	C.	Fernando Alonso
S7	B.	He was run over by a course car
S8	A.	James Hunt
S9	B.	His suspension was broken by a stray camera
S10	B.	Hans Heyer

Surely Not II

S11	A.	Ayrton Senna
S12	C.	He damaged centuries-old stained glass windows
S13	A.	He used a plane to jump fences on a racecourse
S14	C.	Gilles Villeneuve
S15	B.	1950
S16	D.	Watkins Glen
S17	B.	Ayrton Senna
S18	B.	Assault the driver with whom he had collided
S19	A.	Italy
S20	B.	Kimi Raikkonen

Defunct Constructors

79 victories	Team Lotus
35 victories	Brabham
27 victories	Benetton
23 victories	Tyrrell
17 victories	BRM
16 victories	Cooper
9 victories	Maserati
9 victories	Matra
9 victories	Ligier
8 victories	Brawn
4 victories	Jordan
3 victories	Honda
3 victories	March
3 victories	Wolf
2 victories	Lotus F1

1950s Grand Prix Winners

24 wins	Juan Manuel Fangio
13 wins	Alberto Ascari
12 wins	Stirling Moss
6 wins	Tony Brooks
5 wins	Nino Farina
3 wins	Mike Hawthorn
3 wins	Peter Collins
2 wins	José Froilán González
2 wins	Jack Brabham
2 wins	Maurice Trintignant
1 win	Luigi Fagioli
1 win	Piero Taruffi
1 win	Luigi Musso
1 win	Jo Bonnier

Most wins for Scuderia Ferrari

72 wins	Michael Schumacher
15 wins	Niki Lauda
14 wins	Sebastian Vettel
13 wins	Alberto Ascari
11 wins	Felipe Massa
11 wins	Fernando Alonso
10 wins	Kimi Raikkonen
9 wins	Rubens Barrichello
6 wins	Gilles Villeneuve
6 wins	Jack Ickx
5 wins	Alain Prost
5 wins	Gerhard Berger
5 wins	Carlos Reutemann

The Long And The Short

Spa-Francorchamps	7.004 Km/4.352 miles
Silverstone	5.891 Km/3.661 miles
Paul Ricard	5.842 Km/3.630 miles
Suzuka	5.807 Km/3.609 miles
Monza	5.793 Km/3.600 miles
Circuit Of The Americas	5.513 Km/3.426 miles
Marina Bay Street Circuit	5.063 Km/3.146 miles
Hungaroring	4.381 Km/2.722 miles
Red Bull Ring	4.318 Km/2.683 miles
Monaco	3.337 Km/2.074 miles

Most Starts Without A Win

208 starts	Andrea de Cesaris
183 starts	Nick Heidfeld
177 starts	Nico Hulkenberg
176 starts	Sergio Perez
166 starts	Romain Grosjean
165 starts	Martin Brundle
162 starts	Derek Warwick
143 starts	Jean-Pierre Jarier
143 starts	Eddie Cheever
128 starts	Adrian Sutil

First Grands Prix: Countries

Switzerland	1950
Spain	1951
Argentina	1953
USA	1959
Mexico	1963
Austria	1964
Canada	1967
Brazil	1973
Japan	1976
Hungary	1986
Malaysia	1999
Bahrain	2004
Singapore	2008
India	2011
Russia	2014

Most Turbo Wins: 1979-1988

35 wins	French	Alain Prost
14 wins	Brazilian	Ayrton Senna
14 wins	Brazilian	Nelson Piquet
13 wins	English	Nigel Mansell
7 wins	French	René Arnoux
6 wins	Austrian	Niki Lauda
4 wins	Austrian	Gerhard Berger
3 wins	Finnish	Keke Rosberg
3 wins	Italian	Michele Alboreto
2 wins	French	Patrick Tambay
2 wins	Canadian	Gilles Villeneuve
2 wins	French	Didier Pironi
2 wins	French	Jean-Pierre Jabouille
1 win	Italian	Riccardo Patrese
1 win	Italian	Elio de Angelis

Champion With More Than One Team

Four teams: 1950s   Juan Manuel Fangio

Two teams: 1950s, 1960s   Jack Brabham

Two teams: 1960s   Graham Hill

Two teams: 1960s, 1970s   Jackie Stewart

Two teams: 1970s   Emerson Fittipaldi

Two teams: 1970s, 1980s   Niki Lauda

Two teams: 1980s   Nelson Piquet

Two teams: 1980s, 1990s   Alain Prost

Two teams: 1990s, 2000s   Michael Schumacher

Two teams: 2000s, 2010s   Lewis Hamilton

1982 Grand Prix Winners

Ferrari,   2 wins   Didier Pironi

McLaren, 2 wins   Niki Lauda

McLaren, 2 wins   John Watson

Renault,   2 wins   René Arnoux

Renault,   2 wins   Alain Prost

Brabham, 1 win   Riccardo Patrese

Brabham, 1 win   Nelson Piquet

Ferrari,   1 win   Patrick Tambay

Lotus,   1 win   Elio de Angelis

Tyrrell,   1 win   Michele Alboreto

Williams, 1 win   Keke Rosberg

Podiums By US Drivers

19 podiums	Mario Andretti
19 podiums	Dan Gurney
16 podiums	Phil Hill
14 podiums	Richie Ginther
9 podiums	Eddie Cheever
8 podiums	Peter Revson
3 podiums	Masten Gregory
2 podiums	Harry Schell
1 podium	Mark Donohue
1 podium	George Follmer
1 podium	Michael Andretti

Sub-Ten Podium Club 2010-19

8 podiums	Sergio Pérez
3 podiums	Robert Kubica
3 podiums	Daniil Kvyat
1 podium	Sergey Petrov
1 podium	Kamui Kobayashi
1 podium	Nick Heidfeld
1 podium	Carlos Sainz
1 podium	Pierre Gasly
1 podium	Lance Stroll
1 podium	Kevin Magnussen
1 podium	Pastor Maldonado
1 podium	Michael Schumacher

The Runners-Up

1954	José Froilán González
1955/56/57/58	Stirling Moss
1959	Tony Brooks
1960	Bruce McLaren
1961	Wolfgang Von Trips
1969, 1970	Jacky Ickx
1974	Clay Regazzoni
1971, 1978	Ronnie Peterson
1979	Gilles Villeneuve
1981	Carlos Reutemann
1982	Didier Pironi
1985	Michele Alboreto
1992	Riccardo Patrese
1997	Heinz-Harald Frentzen*
1999	Eddie Irvine
2001	David Coulthard
2002, 2004	Rubens Barrichello
2008	Felipe Massa
2019	Vallteri Bottas

130

*Michael Schumacher scored more points than Frenzten but was disqualified from the championship standings after he deliberately collided with championship rival Jacques Villeneuve in the final race of the season.

Part Three: The Stories Behind The Answers

Quizzes are fun, but they're even better when they inform as well as entertain.

With that in mind, this section contains stories (for want of a better word) that in some way relate to each of the 201 multiple-choice questions and/or the answers to them.

Some of the stories are brief, others rather less so. Between them, they cover a wide range of human experience – victory, defeat, joy, despair, comedy, drama, pathos and (although the book doesn't dwell on it) tragedy, and all in the context of the world's best open-wheel motor racing series.

1950 to 1959

1950

Which circuit hosted the first ever Formula One Grand Prix?

B. Silverstone

The first World Championship Grand Prix took place on a sunny day at Silverstone, a former RAF operational training station, on 13th May, 1950.

Twenty-one cars qualified for the race, which was run over 70 laps of a 2.89 mile circuit, the basic layout of which remained largely the same until 1991.

Alfa Romeo's Nino Farina won the race from pole position and also set the fastest race lap. He won two more Grands Prix that season en route to becoming the first F1 World Drivers' Champion.

1951

In how many Grands Prix were podium finishes achieved by non-Italian cars?

B.   None

Of the eight rounds which comprised the 1951 championship, seven were contested in Europe. The other round was the Indianapolis 500, which was neither a Grand Prix nor was contested by the European teams.

In the seven European rounds, Ferrari and Alfa Romeo took all of the 21 podium positions available.

The best finish that a non-Italian car could muster was the fourth place achieved by Louis Rosier's Talbot-Lago at the Belgian Grand Prix, and even then he was more than a lap behind the car in third place.

1952

Who missed the entire 1952 Formula One season through injury?

C.   Juan Manuel Fangio

1952 was a season of change in Formula One, with both it and the 1953 season being run according to Formula 2 rules.

Moreover, the hitherto dominant Alfa Romeo team did not contest the championship, having withdrawn for financial reasons. It would be 27 years before it returned as a constructor.

With Alfa Romeo having pulled out, the reigning world champion, Juan-Manuel Fangio, agreed to defend his title in a Maserati. But as Maserati's new car was not ready, Fangio drove in some non-championship races for BRM.

One of those races was the Tourist Trophy at Dundrod in Northern Ireland. That wasn't in itself an issue, but Fangio had also agreed to drive for Maserati in a non-championship race at Monza the following day. This posed certain logistical issues, which Fangio thought he had overcome by arranging to fly to Milan after the race with Prince Bira of Siam in the latter's private plane.

Bira, however, left early for Italy, leaving Fangio to make alternative travel arrangements. That should have been simple enough, but bad weather meant that he was only able to travel as far as Paris by aircraft. From there, he shared a car to Lyon with fellow driver, Louis Rosier. He then made his way, in Rosier's car, to Monza, arriving at the circuit, exhausted, about 30 minutes before the start of his race.

Perhaps unsurprisingly, he crashed out of the race in the early stages, fracturing vertebrae in his neck. Although he made a full recovery from his injuries, the nature of them and the length of the recovery process meant that he had to sit out the rest of the season.

1953

Which Grand Prix became the first true fly-away Grand Prix in 1953?

D.   Argentinian

The 1953 Argentinian Grand Prix was the first world championship Grand Prix held outside of Europe. To the delight of the locals, who turned up in huge numbers, Fangio qualified on the front row.

With so many people lining the edge of the track and a general air of unruliness, there was concern amongst the drivers about the wisdom of starting the race. These concerns were, however, outweighed by fears that postponing or cancelling it might result in a riot.

As it transpired, the concerns about going ahead with the race proved to be tragically well-founded: a spectator strayed onto the circuit on lap 31, causing Nino Farina to take evasive action. In doing so, Farina lost control of his car, which left the track and hit a number of spectators, thirteen of whom were killed. The race was not stopped, however, and ran the full distance, with Ascari taking the emptiest of victories.

1954

Alberto Ascari drove for Ferrari, Lancia and which other team in 1954?

C.   Maserati

Following a dispute over his salary, Ascari parted company with Ferrari at the end of the 1953 season. He signed for the new Lancia team for the 1954 season, but their first F1 car, the Vittorio Jano-designed D50, was not ready.

Unable to provide him with a car, Lancia permitted Ascari to drive for Maserati in two Grands Prix and for Ferrari in another. He finally got his hands on the D50 in time to take part in the final race of the season, the Spanish Grand Prix. But although he took pole position and led from the start, Ascari's race lasted a mere ten laps before his clutch gave up.

135

He stayed with the team for 1955 but was killed early in the season when testing a Ferrari sports car at Monza.

1955

At which circuit did Stirling Moss notch his first Grand Prix victory?

A.   Aintree

Moss led home Mercedes-Benz team-mate Fangio to win by 0.2 seconds.

With Fangio having had the better of the less experienced Moss that season, there were suggestions that he'd allowed the Briton to win his home Grand Prix. Fangio, however, dismissed such notions, stating that Moss had simply been faster than him.

Moss only drove in one more Grand Prix for Mercedes, who withdrew from motorsport at the end of that season following the death of Pierre Levegh and 83 spectators at the Le Mans 24 Hours.

As for Aintree, it would go on to host the British Grand Prix on four further occasions between 1957 and 1962. Although the full Grand Prix circuit ceased to be used in 1964, the shorter Club circuit still exists and remains in use for sprints and track days as well as motorcycle racing.

1956

Peter Collins gave up his championship chances by doing what at Monza?

B.   He handed over his car to Fangio

With Fangio out of the race, his car having a suffered a broken steering arm, Peter Collins, then lying second in the race, found himself in with a strong chance of winning the championship. But instead of concentrating on chasing the race win and extra point for fastest lap that would bring him the title, he stopped and allowed Fangio to take over his car, an act of selflessness that cost him his best chance of becoming champion.

It wasn't the only time that Collins shared his car with Fangio that season, having done so at Monaco in near-identical circumstances, the duo again sharing the points for second place. Fangio also took over Luigi Musso's car in the season-opening Argentinian Grand Prix and went on to win the race. He and Musso therefore shared the victory, with each man taking four of the eight world championship points awarded for it.

At Monza, however, Musso declined to hand his car over to Fangio. Given that Musso wasn't in contention for the world championship, it makes Collins' decision to give up his car all the more remarkable.

As it turned out, the destiny of the 1956 world championship was decided by the points Fangio gained (and, on two occasions, Collins lost) by taking over his team-mates' cars. Had there been no sharing of cars (and therefore of points), Peter Collins would have been world champion, even allowing for the three points he himself gained through taking second place at Silverstone in a car that he'd taken over from Fon de Portago.

Collins continued to race for Ferrari in Formula One, winning the 1958 British Grand Prix but was killed two weeks later at the Nürburgring.

1957

Which circuit became the longest ever to be used for a Grand Prix?

C.   Pescara, Italy

At 16.032 miles, the Pescara circuit was over a mile longer than the Nürburgring Nordschleife and almost twice as long as Spa-Francorchamps.

The circuit, based entirely on public roads, had been used for motorsport since 1924. The 1957 Pescara Grand Prix was, however, the first time that it hosted a world championship race. That it got the opportunity to do so was due to several Grands Prix having been cancelled that season for financial reasons.

Over 200,000 spectators turned up to watch the Grand Prix in spite of Ferrari having entered only a single car, for Luigi Musso.

The race itself came down to a straight fight between Fangio, then celebrating his fifth world championship, and Stirling Moss. Fangio took pole position but Moss, from second on the grid, turned the tables in the race and took a convincing victory.

Pescara never again hosted a Grand Prix, although a round of the World Sportscar Championship was held there in 1961, after which concerns over safety brought an end to its days as a circuit.

1958

In this year, who became the first British world champion?

C.   Mike Hawthorn

After Pescara appeared on the calendar in 1957, the following year saw another new circuit – at Ain Diab near Casablanca - make its Grand Prix debut.

The race itself was a classic cat-and-mouse affair, with Stirling Moss requiring the F1 equivalent of snookers in order to overhaul Mike Hawthorn's championship lead.

Moss did everything in his power to win the championship, dominating the race and setting fastest lap. And for a time it looked like his efforts would be enough, with Hawthorn, who needed to finish second to clinch the championship if Moss won the race, down in fourth place behind both his own Ferrari team-mate, Phil Hill, and Moss's Vanwall team-mate, Tony Brooks.

That changed, however, when Brooks' Vanwall retired from the race on lap 30. With Brooks gone, Hill followed team orders and allowed Hawthorn past, thereby ensuring that the 'Farnham Flyer' took the second place he needed to become Britain's first world champion.

Having reached the very pinnacle of the sport, Hawthorn immediately retired from motor racing. Tragically, he was killed just three months later in a car crash on the Guildford by-pass.

1959

Who scored BRM's first Grand Prix win?

D.   Jo Bonnier

In a Formula One career that saw Sweden's Jo Bonnier start 104 Grands Prix between 1956 and 1971, he took only one podium – his victory at the wheel of a BRM in the 1959 Dutch Grand Prix.

Bonnier's win was not only the first Grand Prix victory for BRM but also the team's only win with a front-engined car and four-cylinder engine.

Bonnier achieved much greater success in sportscar racing, winning the Targa Florio twice as well as the Sebring 12 Hours and the Nürburgring 1000 km. He also finished second in the Le Mans 24 Hours and, later, won the European 2-Litre Sportscar Championship.

He died as a result of a crash during the 1972 Le Mans 24 Hours, when his self-entered Lola T280 collided with a Ferrari Daytona on the approach to Indianapolis corner.

An intelligent man who spoke six languages, Bonnier spent eight years as President of the Grand Prix Drivers' Association, during which he became a prominent advocate and campaigner for improved circuit safety; indeed, it was in this role that he made his most significant contribution to motorsport.

1960 to 1969

1960

Who scored the first Grand Prix victory for Lotus as a constructor?

C.   Stirling Moss

The first Grand Prix victory for a Lotus car was achieved not by Team Lotus but by Rob Walker's privately run team. It came when Stirling Moss took Walker's Lotus 18 to victory at the 1960 Monaco Grand Prix.

Moss would win three more Grands Prix in Walker's Lotus (one in 1960, two in 1961) before Innes Ireland took Team Lotus's first Grand Prix victory in the final race of the 1961 season.

1961

What was unique (at the time) about the 1961 Dutch Grand Prix?

B.   Every car was running at the finish

There were at least three notable 'firsts' in the 1961 Dutch Grand Prix, it being the first Grand Prix in which every car that started was classified as a finisher; the first in which no pit stops were made during the race; and the first in which Team Lotus's rising star, Jim Clark, finished in a podium position.

1962

For which constructor did Dan Gurney score their only Grand Prix win?

A.   Porsche

Dan Gurney had a knack for taking maiden Grand Prix wins for constructors: in addition to Porsche, he scored the first Grand Prix victories for both Brabham and Eagle. Indeed, three of his four Grand Prix wins were 'first victories'.

In a long and distinguished career, he also won the Le Mans 24 Hours, took several victories in both NASCAR and IndyCar racing and twice finished second in the Indianapolis 500. In addition, he achieved success as a constructor, invented the 'Gurney flap', and is credited with having started the custom of spraying champagne from the podium, having first done so after taking victory at Le Mans in 1967.

1963

In which 1963 Grand Prix did Jim Clark lap every other finisher?

D.   Dutch

Having come agonisingly close to winning the world championship in 1962, Jim Clark utterly dominated Formula One in 1963. He won seven of the season's ten Grands Prix, usually at a canter.

Such was his margin of superiority that he came very close to winning by a lap (8.7 miles) at Spa. He duly did so at the very next race, the Dutch Grand Prix at Zandvoort.

1964

At which circuit did Ferrari's Lorenzo Bandini take his sole Grand Prix victory?

A.   Zeltweg Airfield

The Zeltweg airfield circuit hosted the first ever Austrian Grand Prix in 1964.

The circuit's concrete surface was, however, more than slightly uneven. So much so, in fact, that most of the principal contenders for victory – Jim Clark, Dan Gurney and John Surtees - dropped out of the race before half-distance with either suspension or drivetrain problems. Pole-sitter Graham

Hill also retired early on, leaving the way open for Lorenzo Bandini to take victory.

Zeltweg never again hosted a Grand Prix. Indeed, six years would pass before Austria returned to the F1 calendar.

Bandini's win at Zeltweg would remain his only Grand Prix victory, although he scored several more podium finishes in F1, all at the wheel of a Ferrari, before his untimely death at Monaco in 1967.

1965

Why did Jim Clark miss the 1965 Monaco Grand Prix?

B.   He was in the USA

Although Jim Clark took four pole positions at Monaco (1962, 1963, 1964 and 1966), he never won round the streets of the principality.

1965 might have been the year to change that, but with Lotus having mounted an assault on the Indianapolis 500, Clark found himself over 4500 miles from Monaco during the Grand Prix weekend. It mattered not, as he went on to win both the '500' and the F1 World Championship that season – a feat that remains unmatched over 50 years later.

In more recent times (2017), Fernando Alonso skipped the Monaco Grand Prix to take part in qualifying at Indianapolis, albeit his endeavours were less successful than those of Clark.

1966

Who scored the only Grand Prix win for a car powered by a 16-cylinder engine?

D.   Jim Clark

BRM hedged their bets regarding the introduction of the new F1 engine

142

regulations for the 1966 season, which saw the maximum engine capacity double from 1.5 litres to 3.0 litres.

Two different engine options were explored by the Bourne marque – an H16 engine (essentially two vertically stacked flat 8 engines) and a V12 unit, the latter being developed in partnership with Harry Weslake.

Ultimately, BRM chose the H16 engine. Complex, overweight and with a narrow power band, it was a flop.

It says much that the combined talents of Clark (in a BRM-powered Lotus), Stewart and Hill could amass but one victory between them. Typically, it fell to Clark, the H16 in his Lotus 43 somehow holding together until the end of the United States Grand Prix.

The H16 engine continued to be used, principally by BRM, in 1967. It took no further Grand Prix wins and just one podium, Jackie Stewart's second place in the Belgian Grand Prix.

1967

At which Grand Prix did the Ford Cosworth DFV engine make its debut?

B.   Dutch

When Jim Clark strode to victory at Zandvoort in 1967 (having never sat in the Lotus 49 until practice started), no-one could have known that it marked the beginning of an era in which the DFV engine (funded by Ford, designed and built by Cosworth) would power drivers to twelve world championships, 154 Grands Prix wins, two victories in the Le Mans 24 Hours and, later, over 60 wins in Formula 3000.

The DFV also gave rise to a family of racing engines, the most successful of which was the DFX, a 2.65 litre turbocharged engine that utterly dominated IndyCar racing for a decade.

Oh, and if you're wondering what 'DFV' stands for, it's Double Four

143

Valve. This is because it has two banks of four cylinders, with each cylinder having four valves.

1968

Who became the first driver to use a full-face crash helmet in a Grand Prix?

C.   Dan Gurney

At 1.93 metres, Dan Gurney was tall for a racing driver. Indeed, his height meant that his head often protruded well out of the cockpit and above such protection as might be offered by the windscreen/air deflector (and even that of the roll-over bar), with the result that his face was often struck by flying debris. Little wonder, then, that he personally developed a variety of protective masks throughout the 1960s.

Gurney's search for a truly effective face protector finally bore fruit when he attended a dirt track motorcycle race. Having noted that the dirt track riders wore full-face helmets to shield their faces from the cascade of debris thrown up by riders in front, Gurney thereafter teamed up with Bell Helmets to develop a full-face helmet suitable for use in single-seat racing cars. He first wore the resulting design at Indianapolis in 1968 and thereafter at the German Grand Prix.

Within a short time, full-face helmets were *de rigueur* in many forms of motorsport. Bell did not, however, reap the full harvest that their efforts merited – for some reason they omitted to patent their design!

1969

In a season dominated by Jackie Stewart, which other driver also led over 100 race laps?

D.   Jochen Rindt

He may only have won a single Grand Prix and finished fourth in the points standings that season, but Rindt led nearly three times as many laps as championship runner-up Ickx, and over three times as many as fellow Grand Prix winners Hill and Hulme.

Jackie Stewart was, however, the class of the field in 1969. He won six Grands Prix and led more than twice as many laps as Rindt. Such was the margin of his dominance that, with better reliability, Stewart could easily have won eight or nine of the championship's eleven rounds that season.

1970 - 1979

1970

Who won the first Grand Prix of the new decade?

A.   Jack Brabham

Jack Brabham was 44 years old when he retired from motorsport at the end of the 1970 season, but his form in the first half of the season was such that he could count himself unlucky to have mounted the top step of the podium just once.

He came within a few hundred yards of victory at both Monaco, where he locked up his brakes at the final corner and slid straight on, and Brands Hatch, where his Brabham ran out of fuel with the finish line in sight.

Jochen Rindt was the beneficiary on both occasions, and as it transpired the extra six points gained by him were just enough to ensure that he won the world championship. Tragically, it was a posthumous victory, the only one in the sport's history, as Rindt had succumbed to injuries sustained in practice at Monza.

1971

At the Italian Grand Prix, what was the gap between winner Peter Gethin and fifth place man Howden Ganley?

B.   0.61 seconds

There was a time when Monza, even more so than today, was a veritable cathedral of speed: a fast-flowing mixture of straights and curves with nary a hairpin nor chicane to interrupt progress.

It lent itself to races – the renowned 'Monza slipstreamers' - in which lines of cars would tour the circuit at high speed, swapping places lap after lap as their drivers vied to put themselves into the right position for the last lap charge out of Parabolica to the finishing line. That era came to an end in 1972, when the addition of two chicanes for safety reasons broke the flow of the circuit and lowered the average lap speed by around 20 miles per hour.

The old era departed, however, in a blaze of glory – the 1971 Italian Grand Prix was a classic slipstreaming race that saw BRM's Peter Gethin take his only Grand Prix victory, beating rising Swedish star, Ronnie Peterson, by 0.01 seconds. Indeed, the gap between Gethin and his team-mate Howden Ganley, who was fifth, was just 0.61 seconds.

Gethin's average speed that day was 150.75 miles per hour. It would take 32 years before anyone won a Grand Prix at a higher average speed. Fittingly, it would be at Monza, chicanes and all.

1972

Who scored BRM's final Grand Prix win?

A.   Jean-Pierre Beltoise

Jean-Pierre Beltoise was at a physical disadvantage for most of his racing career, having never regained the full range of movement in his left arm after a crash in 1962. As a consequence, his best performances often came in races in which wet weather reduced the cornering loads and thereby enabled him to compete on a more even footing.

The 1972 Monaco Grand Prix was one such example. Having qualified fourth in his BRM, Beltoise took the lead on the first lap and was never headed during the two and a half hours which it took to complete the race distance.

His performance was all the more impressive for the fact that he beat Ferrari's Jacky Ickx, a driver renowned for his prowess in wet weather, into second place. It was the only Grand Prix victory of Beltoise's career, although he would win again for BRM in the non-championship World Championship Victory Race held at Brands Hatch at the end of the season.

Beltoise also scored BRM's last podium position in F1, taking second place at the 1974 South African Grand Prix. By then, however, BRM was in sharp decline. Having lost its main backer, the Owen Organisation, at the end of 1974, the team continued to race in F1 under the Stanley-BRM banner but ceased to participate in the F1 World Championship after a disastrous 1977 season.

Oh, and if you're wondering if Helmut Marko drove for BRM in F1, the answer is that he did. Unfortunately, his nascent career (he won the Le Mans 24 Hours in 1971) was curtailed when a stone penetrated his visor at the 1972 French Grand Prix, resulting in him losing the sight in his left eye.

1973

Jackie Stewart retired at the end of this season, having started how many Grands Prix?

D.   99

Had fate not been so cruel, Jackie Stewart would have retired at the end of the 1973 United States Grand Prix, having started exactly 100 Grands Prix.

Alas, Francois Cevert (Stewart's team-mate and close friend) was killed during practice at Watkins Glen, the result being that the two remaining Tyrrells (that of Stewart and Chris Amon) were withdrawn from the race.

Stewart departed F1 as a triple world champion who had done, and thereafter continued to do, much to improve the safety of the sport. His crusade for safety, which included leading several boycotts of circuits, made him unpopular in certain quarters, a fact that Stewart himself later acknowledged. As he put it, "I would have been a much more popular World Champion if I had always said what people wanted to hear. I might have been dead, but definitely more popular."

148

Now aged 80, he is the last surviving F1 world champion from the 1960s.

1974

How many drivers notched their first Grand Prix victory in the 1974 season?

A.   Three

Although 1974 started with a former world champion, Denny Hulme, taking his final Grand Prix victory, it also saw two future world champions score their first F1 victories.

Those two drivers, Niki Lauda and Jody Scheckter, would both later win the world championship for Ferrari. For Lauda in particular, the 1974 season saw a dramatic upturn in his fortunes, going as he did from someone who had scored just two championship points in two seasons of F1 to the leader of a resurgent Ferrari team bound for championship glory.

The third 'new winner' of 1974 was Carlos Reutemann. He too would go on to win Grands Prix for Ferrari but would come closest to world championship success for Williams, losing out on the 1981 championship in the last race of the season.

1975

What did Vittorio Brambilla do immediately after winning the rain-shortened Austrian Grand Prix?

B.   Slide into a crash barrier.

Although scheduled to run for 54 laps, torrential rain caused the race to be stopped after just over half that distance. Brambilla, who was leading comfortably in his March, was astonished to see the chequered flag shown so early in the race.

Realising that he'd just taken his first (and, as it turned out, only) Grand

Prix win, he lifted both hands off the steering wheel in celebration, only for his car to slide into a crash barrier. Although his car's nosecone was somewhat askew, it remained driveable and he was able to complete his victory lap without further incident.

1976

How many Grands Prix did Niki Lauda win in 1976 before his accident at the Nürburgring?

A.   Five.

Lauda won in Brazil, South Africa, Belgium, Monaco and (controversially) Britain to give him a championship lead of 31 points (and 35 over eventual champion James Hunt) going into the German Grand Prix.

He missed two Grands Prix after his accident at the Nürburgring but returned, his burns not yet fully healed, at the Italian Grand Prix. He finished a remarkable fourth in that race and went one place better at Watkins Glen.

He was still leading the championship race going into the final race of the season, the Japanese Grand Prix at Fuji. The race was, however, run in appalling weather conditions, which put Lauda at a disadvantage on account of the injuries he had sustained in Germany.

In particular, a damaged tear duct caused tears to stream from one of his eyes, impairing his vision. With no way of being able to stem the tears, Lauda took the brave – and undoubtedly correct – decision to retire from the race.

Moreover, in all the drama that surrounded that season, and that race in particular, it's often forgotten that three other drivers, including former world champion Emerson Fittipaldi, also pulled into the pits and retired from the race because of the conditions.

1977

In which Grand Prix did Jacques Laffite score his and Ligier's first victory in F1?

D.   Swedish

The 1977 season was largely a story of Ferrari (and Lauda) consistency and Lotus misfortune, and the Swedish Grand Prix was a prime example of the latter.

Having taken pole position in his Lotus 78 'wing car', Mario Andretti showed the rest of the field a clean pair of heels. Conscious that the 'development' engines used by Lotus that season (to try to counter the 78's lack of straight-line speed) were somewhat fragile, Andretti took pains to try to preserve his engine.

Unfortunately, although his DFV made it to the end of the race, it had been running rich and using too much fuel. A surprised Andretti therefore had to make a late-race pit stop to take on extra fuel. This cost him an entire lap and left the way open for Jacques Laffite to take the win in his Ligier-Matra.

Laffite thus became the first French driver to win a Grand Prix in a French car powered by a French engine. He would go on to win five more Grands Prix in his career, all at the wheel of a Ligier.

1978

Which team was sued by another team over the design of its 1978 F1 car?

C.   Arrows

The Arrows F1 team was founded in 1977 by a consortium which included former Shadow designers Tony Southgate and Dave Wass.

It was therefore perhaps no great surprise that the first Arrows F1 car, the FA1, bore a close resemblance to Shadow's new car, the DN9. Too close, as it happened, and Shadow sued for copyright infringement.

Knowing that their prospects of successfully defending the court action were slim, Arrows hurriedly designed and built a new car, the A1, in a little over seven weeks. It was just as well that they did so, as they lost the court case and were thereafter prohibited from racing the FA1.

And that wasn't the only drama for Arrows in 1978: co-founder Franco Ambrosio was jailed in Italy early that year, and driver Riccardo Patrese was unjustly blamed for causing the startline pile-up at Monza that resulted in the death of Lotus's Ronnie Peterson.

Arrows continued to race in F1 until the end of the 2002 season, starting 382 Grands Prix without scoring a Grand Prix win.

1979

The French Grand Prix featured a memorable scrap for second place. Who won the race?

B.   Jean-Pierre Jabouille

Whilst the eyes of the world were understandably on the titanic battle for second place between Gilles Villeneuve and René Arnoux, it was Arnoux's Renault team-mate, Jean-Pierre Jabouille, who took victory.

Jabouille's win was not merely his first Grand Prix victory, it was also the first for a turbocharged car. Moreover, it was the first Grand Prix win for a French driver in a French car powered by a French engine using French fuel **and** running on French tyres. It also happened to be Renault's first win in F1, and it happened in France.

Some things are just meant to be.

1980 - 1989

1980

Which Grand Prix was subsequently downgraded to a non-championship race?

C.   Spain

Formula One found itself embroiled in a civil war in the early 1980s. On one side, there was FISA, the sport's governing body, and on the other there was the Formula One Constructors Association ('FOCA'), of which all of the teams bar Ferrari, Renault and Alfa Romeo were members.

The 1980 Spanish Grand Prix was the first major casualty of the conflict. The immediate cause lay in FISA's decision to fine a number of drivers from FOCA teams for failing to attend pre-race briefings in Belgium and Monaco; FISA claimed that the briefings were mandatory, but FOCA's lawyers argued that they were not. When the fines weren't paid, FISA ordered the suspension of the defaulting drivers' racing licences. In response, the FOCA teams threatened to withdraw from the Spanish Grand Prix.

The promoters of the Spanish Grand Prix offered to pay a deposit on the drivers' outstanding fines, but FISA insisted that the fines be paid by the drivers themselves. King Juan Carlos of Spain then became involved, demanding that the race go ahead.

Whilst this was going on, only the Ferrari, Renault and Alfa Romeo teams took part in the first practice session. The session was, however, halted after only 30 minutes.

Practice eventually resumed, but only after the race organisers, having decided to bypass FISA, ejected FISA officials from the circuit.

The upshot of this was that Ferrari, Alfa Romeo and Renault packed up and went home, leaving the race to be contested by only the FOCA teams, save for Osella, who 'loaned' their cars to their sponsors and competed in the race under that guise.

The race itself was one of attrition, with only six cars being classified as finishers. As FISA subsequently declared the race to have been illegal, the results did not count towards the championship.

This had no effect on the outcome of that year's championship but did have the unfortunate consequence of depriving Ensign's Patrick Gaillard of the only world championship point won by him in his career.

The FISA/FOCA conflict continued to blight the sport for some time to come, the consequences of which included a drivers' strike in 1982 and a FOCA-organised boycott of that year's San Marino Grand Prix.

1981

What team scored the first Grand Prix win for a car with a wholly carbonfibre monocoque?

B.   McLaren

With Ron Dennis now at the helm, McLaren became the first team to fully embrace the use of carbonfibre.

McLaren engineer Steve Nichols, who had previously worked in the aerospace industry, suggested that carbonfibre would be a suitable material from which to construct the monocoque of an F1 car, it being both light and strong. His suggestion was accepted, and McLaren duly built their new F1 car, the MP4-1, around a carbonfibre monocoque using carbon supplied by Nichols's former employer, Hercules Aerospace.

Although the MP4-1 took only one Grand Prix victory, the 1981 British Grand Prix, it pointed the way ahead for F1 design and construction (John Watson's huge accident at Monza that season provided convincing evidence of its strength), and it was soon adopted by every other team.

1982

Which driver won the 1982 Brazilian Grand Prix on the road only to later be disqualified?

C.   Nelson Piquet

By 1982, a turbocharged engine was the thing to have in F1. However, only the Ferrari, Renault and (later that season) the Brabham and Toleman teams had them.

In a bid to counter their power disadvantage relative to the turbos, several Ford-powered teams took advantage of a badly drafted regulation which allowed cars to be topped up with normal lubricants and fluids after the race before being weighed.

They did this by fitting their cars with large water tanks, ostensibly to provide cooling for the brakes. In reality, however, the purpose of these tanks was to enable cars so equipped to run for most of the race much lighter than they ought to have been.

Although the 'water tank' cars started the race with their tanks full, they wasted little time in emptying them once the race began. The effect of this was they carried about 30 kilogrammes less weight than they should have, with consequent benefits in terms of performance, tyre wear and brake life. At the end of the race they refilled their water tanks, thereby ensuring that they complied with the minimum weight limit at post-race scrutineering.

It was a clever idea, but FISA acted quickly to stamp it out, disqualifying both Piquet and Rosberg from the Brazilian Grand Prix. Curiously, though, other drivers whose cars had exactly the same system went unpunished, to the extent that they profited from the exclusion of Piquet and Rosberg.

The regulations were then changed so that the post-race topping up of 'coolants' was no longer permitted. This resulted in yet another dispute arising between the FOCA teams, they having been the ones who exploited the water tank loophole, and FISA. In consequence of this, most of the FOCA teams boycotted the San Marino Grand Prix. The race went ahead without them, however, and counted towards the world championship.

1983

In what position did race-winner John Watson qualify for the 1983 US (West) Grand Prix?

A.   22nd

This wasn't Watson's only win from the nether recesses of the grid: he had won the 1982 US Grand Prix, held in Detroit, from a starting position of 17th. Indeed, in some ways, his win in Detroit – in which he'd overtaken car after car in a remorseless charge to the front, having switched to harder compound tyres when the race was red-flagged after six laps – was the best of his career.

At Long Beach, however, Watson's skill and the durability of his Michelin tyres were given something of a helping hand by fate, in the form of two collisions which, in successive laps, took out three of the race-leading quartet.

It was, however, to be the last of Watson's five Grand Prix victories, for he found himself out of a drive at the end of the season, when Alain Prost, having been sacked by Renault, was snapped up by McLaren to partner Niki Lauda.

That was hard on Watson, but perhaps he can take some solace in the fact that to this day no-one else has ever won a Grand Prix from such a lowly starting position.

1984

Which future world champion crashed out of the lead of the 1984 Monaco Grand Prix?

B.   Nigel Mansell

Having qualified second in his Lotus-Renault, Mansell overtook Prost for the lead on the ninth lap of the race and promptly pulled away at around two seconds per lap.

It was the first time Mansell had led a Grand Prix, but it wasn't to last. Pushing a little too hard in the very wet conditions, his Lotus ran over a painted white road marking on the run up to *Casino Square*, causing it to snap out of control and strike a crash barrier.

The race was eventually stopped after just over an hour, with Prost taking the win ahead of two impressive newcomers to F1: Ayrton Senna and Stefan Bellof.

Mansell's crash enraged Lotus team manager Peter Warr, who some time later stated that Mansell "would never win a Grand Prix as long as I have a hole in my a**e" - a prediction that did not, of course, date well!

1985

Who finished third in Australia in spite of having only three working wheels at the end of the race?

C.   Philippe Streiff

Ligier's prospects for a successful 1985 Australian Grand Prix seemed pretty remote on race morning, with Philippe Streiff and Jacques Laffite having respectively qualified in 18th and 20th places.

As it turned out, however, a high rate of attrition meant that the two Ligiers found themselves running second and third late in the race, with

157

Streiff right on Laffite's heels. He ought perhaps to have stayed there, but the lure of second place was just too much for him to resist. Unfortunately, his attempt to pass his team-leader on the penultimate lap was a clumsy effort that resulted in his front left wheel making contact with the rear of Laffite's car, damaging both.

Luckily, both cars were able to make it to the chequered flag without losing their podium places, albeit the front left wheel of Streiff's car was barely attached to the car and not at all to the steering rack.

Streiff had been hoping to secure a drive with Ligier for 1986, but his collision with Laffite put paid to those chances. Instead, he went on to drive for Tyrrell and AGS in F1 before severe injuries resulting from a testing crash at Brazil in 1989 ended his career.

1986

What was unique (at the time) about the 1986 F1 season?

B.   Only turbocharged engines were permitted

The 'turbo revolution' started by Renault in 1977 reached its zenith in 1986, with the engine regulations permitting only the use of turbocharged engines with a capacity of up to 1500cc.

It achieved little: costs went up for the smaller teams but their chances of victory remained much as before – negligible. The 'turbo-only' rule lasted just one season, with normally aspirated cars permitted to return in 1987.

Turbochargers were banned after the 1988 season but returned in 2014 when new engine regulations came into effect.

1987

Who won the Jim Clark Trophy?

B.   Jonathan Palmer

With turbocharged engines set to be outlawed from 1989, normally aspirated engines made a return in 1987, but this time in 3.5 litre form. But even with an extra 500cc over the previous maximum capacity of 3 litres, a car powered by a normally aspirated engine simply couldn't hope to compete for outright victory.

Recognising this gulf in performance, the FIA introduced two new competitions for competitors using normally aspirated engines: the Jim Clark Trophy for drivers, and the Colin Chapman Trophy for constructors.

As it transpired, only the Tyrrell team ran two normally aspirated cars for the whole season. Accordingly, they won the Colin Chapman Trophy with ease, and their drivers, Jonathan Palmer and Philippe Streiff, finished first and second in the battle for the Jim Clark Trophy.

Twelve of the eighteen teams ran normally aspirated engines in 1988, but although none were able to compete for outright race victories the FIA decided that the Jim Clark and Colin Chapman Trophies would not be contested that year. Indeed, as of 2020 they have not been reintroduced in any form.

1988

Who collided with Senna at Monza, thus ending McLaren's chances of winning every Grand Prix that season?

A.   Jean-Louis Schlesser

With Nigel Mansell absent through illness, Williams called upon Jean-Louis Schlesser to take the Englishman's place at Monza.

About to celebrate his 40th birthday, Schlesser had made only one previous attempt to qualify for a Grand Prix, some five years previously. He hadn't qualified then, but he made it onto the grid this time, albeit in a lowly 22nd place, some 5 seconds slower than the McLarens that headed the time sheets.

As usual in 1988, the McLarens of Senna and Prost dominated qualifying, but any notion of a 1-2 finish vanished when Prost retired on lap 34 with engine trouble, leaving Senna with a lead of more than half a minute over the Ferraris of Berger and Alboreto.

It might have stayed that way, too, had not Alboreto, perhaps aware that this would his final race at Monza for Ferrari, upped his pace and closed on team-mate Berger. The Austrian responded and the two Ferraris started to eat into Senna's lead, bringing it down to just 5 seconds with three laps to go. And that's when fate – in the guise of Schlesser's Williams - intervened.

With Senna coming up to lap him as they approached the first chicane, Schlesser locked his brakes, causing him to run wide on the entry to the chicane. Senna, expecting Schlesser to stay out of the way, entered the chicane and was negotiating the second part of it when Schlesser speared into him. The Williams struck the right rear wheel of the McLaren, nudging Senna into a spin and out of the race.

To the joy of the Tifosi, Berger and Alboreto strolled home for a wholly unexpected Ferrari 1-2. It was Ferrari's only win of the season, and it came at their home Grand Prix just four weeks after the death of Enzo Ferrari.

It's worth repeating: some things are just meant to be.

1989

Who won the Japanese Grand Prix after Senna was disqualified?

D.   Alessandro Nannini

Having been thwarted in their ambition to win every Grand Prix in 1988, McLaren found themselves facing a stiffer challenge in 1989.

Even so, the fight for the Drivers' World Championship was once again a two-horse race between Senna and Prost. With two Grands Prix to go, Senna trailed Prost in the standings by 16 points in spite of having taken six wins to Prost's four. But thanks to the scoring system then in operation, the Brazilian could still win the championship IF he won the last two Grands Prix of the season, even if Prost finished second to him in both races,

Things started well for him at Suzuka, where he took pole position from Prost by 1.7 seconds. In the race, however, Prost took the lead at the start and built up a small cushion over Senna. The Brazilian fought back but struggled to pass his team-mate, who had chosen a lower downforce set-up to maximise his straightline speed.

With just over six laps to go, Senna attempted to pass Prost into the chicane. Prost refused to yield, and the two cars collided. Prost stopped there and then but Senna rejoined the circuit after being pushed by marshals. He made a pit stop to have a new nosecone fitted and thereafter set about catching and passing the new race leader, Alessandro Nannini.

Senna duly crossed the line first, but his joy was short-lived - he was disqualified for improperly rejoining the circuit, handing the race victory to Nannini and the world championship to Prost.

With Prost about to leave for Ferrari, McLaren appealed the stewards' decision, but no avail. Senna and Prost would collide again at Suzuka the following year, this time rather more dramatically after Senna committed the F1 equivalent of a professional foul on the opening lap.

For Nannini, however, the 1989 Japanese Grand Prix was the sole victory of a career cruelly cut short as a result of severe injuries arising from a helicopter accident.

1990 - 1999

1990

Adrian Newey designed which of the following 1990 F1 cars?

A.   Leyton House CG901

If it seems like Adrian Newey has been around the Formula One scene for a long time, that's because he has.

Having started out with the Fittipaldi Formula One team shortly after graduating in 1980, he moved into other forms of racing (Formula 2, IMSA and IndyCar) with March before being appointed as the Chief Designer of the team's 1988 Formula One car.

That car, the March 881, was the only normally aspirated car to lead a Grand Prix (albeit briefly) in the 1988 season. But with March beset by financial problems, which led to its sale to Japanese businessman Akari Akagi, his 1989 car was rather less successful.

Newey stayed with the team, now renamed Leyton House, for 1990. Unfortunately, his latest car, the CG901, struggled in the early part of the season. This led to his dismissal by the team, although changes he had already made to the car ultimately transformed its performance.

He wasn't out of work for long, however, with Williams securing his services shortly after he left March. The move to Grove was the making of Newey. Working alongside Patrick Head, he played a pivotal role in bringing the glory days back to Williams.

He went on to repeat the feat at McLaren before moving to Red Bull, where he became the first – and so far only - designer to have won the F1 Constructors' Championship with three different teams.

1991

Who won the 1991 Canadian Grand Prix after race-leader Nigel Mansell's Williams ground to a halt on the last lap?

C.   Nelson Piquet

Having led from the start, Mansell had almost a minute in hand over Benetton's Nelson Piquet as he entered the hairpin towards the end of the final lap.   As a delighted Mansell waved to the crowd, his Williams suddenly ground to a halt. In a flash, first became sixth as Piquet strolled to his 23rd and final Grand Prix victory.

Quite what caused Mansell's car to fail was the subject of conjecture: Mansell and Williams both blamed it on a technical issue with the gearbox while some people claimed that he either stalled the engine after letting the revs drop too low when waving to fans or he accidentally hit the engine kill-switch.

Whatever the cause, it was a harsh blow after a terrific drive – one of a series of mishaps that dashed Mansell's hopes of winning the world championship that year.

It would, however, be a different story in 1992.

1992

For which team did Damon Hill make his Grand Prix debut?

A.   Brabham

In spite of being Williams' test driver in 1992, Damon Hill had rather less competitive machinery at his disposal when it came to making his Grand Prix debut.

Having joined the Brabham team after the third Grand Prix of the season, Hill failed to qualify for five races in succession before scraping onto the grid in 26th place at Silverstone. He finished the race in 16th place, four laps down on Nigel Mansell's dominant Williams.

Germany brought another failure to qualify, but Hill got onto the grid in Hungary and finished 11th in the race, the last of the runners and four laps down on the winner. It was the Brabham team's last hurrah; beset by financial woes, it folded after the race.

1993

Who did Mika Hakkinen replace as Ayrton Senna's team-mate at McLaren?

A.   Michael Andretti

Having won the IndyCar series in 1991 and finished runner-up in 1992, taking 13 wins over those two seasons, Michael Andretti's foray into F1 was anticipated with interest.

Unfortunately, a change in regulations limited the number of laps that each driver could complete in practice. This put Andretti, who was unfamiliar with the circuits used by F1, at something of a disadvantage. His difficulties were compounded by the fact that F1 cars were technically more sophisticated than the Indy cars he was used to, and his decision to commute to races and test sessions from the USA rather than move to Europe scarcely helped either. On top of that, Andretti would have to stand direct comparison with his team-mate, a certain Ayrton Senna.

It was too much to expect that he'd shine in such circumstances, and so it proved, with Andretti taking just a single podium (third in the Italian Grand Prix) in his thirteen races. By way of contrast, Senna picked up three wins in those thirteen races and would go on to claim two more victories in the last three Grands Prix that season.

After leaving McLaren and F1, Andretti returned to IndyCar racing, in which he scored a further fourteen race victories over the years and twice finished runner-up in the championship.

1994

Which of the following drivers was NOT suspended from at least one Grand Prix during the 1994 season?

B.   Jean Alesi

No fewer than three drivers were suspended for at least one Grand Prix in 1994.

First on the naughty step was Eddie Irvine, who was initially banned for one race for his part in a four-car crash at the season-opening Brazilian Grand Prix. Irvine appealed that ban, only for the FIA to increase it to three races. Next up was Mika Hakkinen, who received a one race ban after being adjudged to have caused a first lap pile-up in Germany.

And then there was Michael Schumacher. It's fair to say that both Schumacher and his team had a controversial 1994 season. Indeed, the story of their season could fill a book on its own, but for present purposes we'll concentrate simply on Schumacher's two-race ban.

It was initially handed down at Silverstone after he overtook Damon Hill on the formation lap then ignored a black flag. He was permitted to race while the ban was under appeal, during which time he was disqualified from the Belgian Grand Prix after finishing first on the road. Shortly thereafter, he found out that his appeal against the ban imposed at Silverstone had been unsuccessful, the result being that he missed out on the Italian and Portuguese Grands Prix.

As for Alesi, he also missed two Grands Prix in 1994, but in his case it was due to an injury sustained in a testing accident rather than through having incurred the wrath of the race stewards.

1995

With which team did Nigel Mansell end his career as an F1 driver?

D.   McLaren

Having been unable to agree contractual terms to continue racing for Williams in 1993. Nigel Mansell went to the USA and tried his hand in the CART IndyCar championship, signing on with Newman/Haas as team-mate to 1978 F1 World Champion Mario Andretti.

Mansell got off to a flying start, taking pole position and victory in his first ever IndyCar race. He would go on to win four more races that season, and with it the CART IndyCar championship.

As he won the IndyCar championship before that year's F1 world championship had been settled, he became the first – and so far only – man to hold both the Formula One and IndyCar championships at the same time.

He combined a further, less successful, season in IndyCar in 1994 with four stand-in appearances in F1 for Williams. He won the last of those races, the 1994 Australian Grand Prix, but was not offered a race seat with the team for 1995.

He did, however, return to F1 that year, having signed a multi-year deal with McLaren. Unfortunately, his season started badly, the cockpit of the team's new MP4/10 being too narrow for him.

A revised car, the MP4/10B, was produced but in the meantime Mansell missed out on the first two Grands Prix of the season. When he finally made his McLaren debut at Imola, he found the MP4/10B to be somewhat lacking in performance. A mid-race collision with Eddie Irvine forced him to pit, and he came home a disappointing tenth.

Things went no better in the next race, the Spanish Grand Prix, from which he retired due to his car's wayward handling. He and the team parted company shortly thereafter, and although he subsequently tested some F1 cars he never again raced in a Grand Prix.

1996

Whose crash helmet did David Coulthard wear in the Monaco Grand Prix?

B.   Michael Schumacher

Having discovered during the morning warm-up session that the visor on his helmet was misting up in the damp conditions, David Coulthard noted that Michael Schumacher, whose helmet had a double visor, was having no such problems. Sportingly, Schumacher agreed to loan Coulthard one of his spare helmets, which Coulthard duly wore in the Grand Prix.

After finishing second in the race – his best result of the season – Coulthard was permitted by Schumacher to keep the helmet as a memento. With McLaren boss Ron Dennis also keen on acquiring the helmet, Coulthard arranged for a replica to be made for Dennis, although he has since revealed that he waited some time before telling Dennis that he'd been given a replica rather than the real thing!

1997

In which 1997 Grand Prix did the top three in qualifying all set the same time to a thousandth of a second?

D.   European (Jerez)

The 1997 European Grand Prix is largely remembered for Michael Schumacher's clumsy (and failed) attempt to push championship rival Jacques Villeneuve's Williams off the road, but that wasn't the only thing of note to happen that weekend.

With Villeneuve only needing to finish third to win the championship, he allowed the McLarens of Hakkinen and Coulthard, who had swapped places under team orders, to pass him on the final lap, sparking accusations of collusion between the two teams. Hakkinen thus took his first Grand Prix win.

167

And if that wasn't enough drama for one weekend, qualifying threw up an unprecedented situation, in that the fastest three cars – those of Villeneuve, Michael Schumacher and Heinz-Harald Frentzen - all set exactly the same time (1.21.072) to the one-thousandth of a second. Pole position was therefore determined by the order in which the times were set, meaning that Villeneuve, being the first man to set the time, started from pole.

1998

In which 1998 Grand Prix did Michael Schumacher take the chequered flag (and the win) in the pit lane?

C.   British

For much of the 1998 British Grand Prix, it looked highly likely that Mika Hakkinen would be heading home with the winner's trophy and ten valuable world championship points.

But after building up a lead of nearly 50 seconds, the Finn's McLaren spun on the increasingly wet track surface, damaging his front wing. He still led the race but a Safety Car eroded the rest of his margin and made him vulnerable to attack from Schumacher. After the race restarted, another error by Hakkinen enabled Schumacher to take the lead.

And then the real drama started. The stewards imposed a 10 second penalty on Schumacher for passing under the Safety Car, but didn't make it clear whether it was to be implemented by adding ten seconds to the German's time at the end of the race or by requiring him to serve a stop-go penalty.

Ferrari therefore decided to call Schumacher in on the last lap of the race to serve a stop-go penalty. This, however, meant that he crossed the finishing line (in the pit lane) before reaching his pit box to serve the penalty. That being so, it was therefore doubtful that he had served the penalty during the race.

Following the race, Ferrari and (later) McLaren both protested, and the matter ended up before the FIA's International Court of Appeal. The Court of Appeal accepted Ferrari's arguments that that notice of the penalty was given to them six minutes later than specified by the rules and that it failed to specify whether it was a time penalty or a stop-go penalty.

The Court of Appeal also found that although the stewards had clarified after the race that the penalty they sought to impose was a time penalty, it was not competent to impose such a penalty (as distinct from a stop-go penalty) for an incident that had occurred more than 12 laps before the end of the race. Consequently, the penalty was set aside and Schumacher kept the win.

1999

Who won the last Grand Prix of the millennium?

A.   Mika Hakkinen

The 1999 Formula One season was a curious beast.

As in 1998, it looked very much like it would boil down to a season-long battle between Mika Hakkinen and Michael Schumacher. However, Schumacher's accident at Silverstone put paid to that. With his main rival likely to be sidelined for several months, it seemed reasonable to think that Mika would stroll to the title. It did not, however, turn out that way.

Probable wins for Hakkinen at Silverstone, Austria and Germany were respectively lost due to a loose wheel, a misjudged first-lap passing attempt by Coulthard, and pit stop issues followed by a race-ending puncture. A bizarre accident in Italy added to the Finn's woes, and after Schumacher gifted team-mate Eddie Irvine the win in the penultimate race of the season, Mika went into the last race of 1999 trailing Irvine in the championship standings.

As it turned out, however, the Finn saw off both Ferraris at Suzuka, taking both the race win and his second consecutive world championship.

2000 - 2009

2000

What was different about the 2000 British Grand Prix?

B.   It took place in April rather than July

The FIA invited trouble from the weather gods when they decided that the 2000 British Grand Prix should be moved from its usual July slot to one in late April.

That invitation was accepted: heavy rain in the lead-up to the race flooded a number of car parking areas at the circuit, resulting in their temporary closure for repair.

The car parks remained closed until race day, with fans being advised to watch qualifying at home rather than travel to the circuit, as cars would be turned away. Consequently, the attendance for qualifying was down by around 75%.

The car parks re-opened on race day, but chaos nonetheless ensued, with traffic heading to the circuit backed up for an estimated 15 miles in places.

The event returned to its usual July slot in 2001 and has remained there ever since.

2001

For which team did Jean Alesi drive the last five Grands Prix of his F1 career?

A.   Jordan

It's fair to say that Jean Alesi's talent deserved more by way of results than fate granted him. Having sparkled in a Tyrrell and shown flashes of brilliance in a string of V12 Ferraris that sounded wonderful but all too

170

often lacked something in both speed and reliability, his career started to peter out following his move to Benetton for the 1996 season.

It could all have been so different had he taken either of the two opportunities offered to him to join Williams, but instead he ended up with just a single Grand Prix win to his name.

His career is perhaps best remembered as a series of cameos – his battle for the lead with Senna at Phoenix in 1990, his car control on slick tyres at a damp Magny Cours in 1992, taking 14 seconds out of Senna over 2 laps at a wet Barcelona that same year, losing near-certain wins for Ferrari at successive Italian Grands Prix due to technical problems, a spellbinding but ultimately fruitless drive at Suzuka in 1995, two front-row qualifying performances for Sauber, and qualifying his underwhelming Prost 7th, a second and a half faster than team-mate Nick Heidfeld, at Monaco in 2000.

But when it came to the end of the road for his F1 career, fate was at least kind enough to allow him to arrive there in the cockpit of a Jordan, the team for whom he had shone so brightly in Formula 3000 some twelve years previously.

2002

Which British driver raced for Toyota in their debut season in Formula One in 2002?

B.   Allan McNish

There was a time in the late 1980s and early 1990s when it looked very much like Allan McNish's future lay in Formula One.

Having won the Formula Vauxhall Lotus championship in 1988, he went on to finish runner-up in the 1989 British F3 Championship. Moving up to Formula 3000 in 1990, he won twice that season and finished a creditable fourth in the championship.

Although he tested Formula One cars for several teams over the next few seasons, the prospect of a race seat receded somewhat, leading McNish to concentrate on sportscar racing. He won Le Mans for Porsche in 1998, but it wasn't until 2001 and his appointment as the development driver for Toyota's Formula One programme that the door to a Formula One drive opened itself, with a race seat in the team's debut F1 season following in 2002.

Both McNish and team-mate Mika Salo acquitted themselves fairly well throughout that year, but neither retained their seat for 2003.

McNish spent the next season as the Renault F1 team's test driver before once again returning to sportscars. It was a move that paid off, with victories at both Le Mans (three) and Sebring (four) being amongst the highlights of a racing career that ended with him partnering Tom Kristensen and Loic Duval to victory in the FIA World Endurance Championship in 2013.

2003

Who became the youngest-ever Grand Prix winner (at the time) during the 2003 F1 season?

D.   Fernando Alonso

At the age of 22 years and 26 days, Fernando Alonso became the youngest-ever winner of a Grand Prix, thereby breaking a record set by Bruce McLaren in 1959.

He also took an even older record that day, beating Troy Ruttman's 41 year old record as the youngest man to have won a race (the Indianapolis 500) that counted towards the Formula One world championship.

Alonso held those records until 2008, losing them when Sebastian Vettel won the Italian Grand Prix at the age of 21. Vettel in turn lost them to Max Verstappen, whose victory in the 2016 Spanish Grand Prix was achieved at the tender age of 18 years and 228 days.

How long Max will hold them for is anyone's guess, but the chances are that it won't be anything like the same length of time as either McLaren or Ruttman, who remains the youngest-ever winner of the Indianapolis 500.

2004

How many Grands Prix (out of eighteen contested) did Ferrari win in 2004?

A.   Fifteen

For Ferrari, the 2004 season was one to remember.

Michael Schumacher not only took thirteen Grands Prix wins, breaking his own record and setting a new one that has since been equalled but not beaten, but also took his seventh and final world championship. Indeed, his world championship win was his fifth in succession, a record that remains intact to this day.

There was joy too for the Scuderia, who won the constructors' championship for the fourteenth time. Rubens Barrichello also had his most successful world championship campaign, finishing second in the standings after taking two Grand Prix victories.

The other F1 teams didn't have too much to cheer about, although BAR-Honda enjoyed their best year in F1. Although there were no race wins for them to celebrate, the team took second place in the constructors' championship and Jenson Button finished third in the drivers' championship.

2005

Who took Ralf Schumacher's place in qualifying for the United States Grand Prix?

C.   Ricardo Zonta

The fiasco that was the 2005 Indianapolis Grand Prix revolved around one thing: tyres.

If, like the Ferraris, Minardis and Jordans, you were on Bridgestone rubber then you were fine. If, however, you were on Michelins then you ran the risk – as Toyota's Ralf Schumacher found out in practice – of tyre failure at high speed on turn 13, the banked section of track leading onto the main straight.

Michelin flew in different specification tyres, but to no avail – these, too, were vulnerable to the loads placed on them at turn 13. With Michelin unable to guarantee that their tyres could safely withstand more than ten laps of the circuit at racing speed, it was clear that the teams they supplied had a major headache.

Qualifying went ahead, with Toyota's third driver, Ricardo Zonta, standing in for Ralf Schumacher, who was deemed unfit to drive as a result of the severity of his practice crash. And it was a Toyota – that of Jarno Trulli – which took pole position for the race, the team's first.

With over 100,000 fans expected on race day, a number of suggestions as to how the race might be able to proceed, including the insertion of a temporary chicane at turn 13, were discussed. History records that none of the proposed solutions were implemented, with the FIA flatly refusing to agree to the insertion of a temporary chicane.

The race descended into farce when the Michelin runners peeled off the circuit into the pits at the end of the formation lap, leaving the race to be contested by just six cars. Ultimately, Michael Schumacher took Ferrari's only win of the season whilst Jordan's Narain Karthikeyan became the first Indian driver to score a world championship point.

Formula One returned to the 'Brickyard' in 2006 and 2007, without further incident. The damage had been done, however, and reduced attendances resulted in Indianapolis dropping off the F1 calendar after 2007.

2006

What was Michael Schumacher's finishing position in the Brazilian Grand Prix, his last for Ferrari?

D.   Fourth

Michael Schumacher went into his last Grand Prix for Ferrari (and his last for anyone for over three years) with his championship hopes hanging by a thread, courtesy of an engine failure in the preceding Grand Prix at Suzuka.

Trailing Alonso by ten points, all Schumacher could do was try to win the race and hope that his Spanish rival failed to finish in the points. It was a long shot that grew longer still when fuel pressure issues in qualifying meant that the German would line up tenth on the grid. Any lingering hopes that Schumacher entertained were dashed early in the race when a brush with Fisichella's Renault resulted in a puncture and a significant loss of time.

What followed thereafter was one of Schumacher's finest drives – a charge through the field that took him to fourth place. It wasn't enough to bring him his eighth world championship – and wouldn't have been even if Alonso had failed to finish in the points. But as a souvenir of a stellar, albeit often controversial, career it more than passes muster.

2007

With two Grands Prix left, by how many points did Kimi Raikkonen trail Lewis Hamilton in the championship standings?

A.   Seventeen

Kimi Raikkonen's debut season for Ferrari was the proverbial game of two halves. Having won the season-opening Australian Grand Prix with ease, the Finn thereafter endured a six-race spell in which he struggled to find his Ferrari's sweet spot.

The tide turned in France, where he leap-frogged team-mate Massa to take a much-needed win. He won again at Silverstone and took a hat-trick of podium finishes in Hungary, Turkey and Italy. Even so, he still trailed championship leader Hamilton by 18 points going into the last four races.

A win in Belgium reduced the deficit but a major faux pas by Ferrari at Fuji resulted in both Ferraris having to pit early in the race to change from wet tyres to extreme wets. Raikkonen recovered to third, but Hamilton's win meant that the points differential stood at 17 with two races to go.

And then the unthinkable happened. It was McLaren's turn to get things wrong in China, the result being that whilst Raikkonen took a well-judged victory, the state of Hamilton's tyres led to his race ending in a gravel trap. Even so, Raikkonen went to Interlagos still trailing both Hamilton and his McLaren team-mate Alonso in the points standings.

Hamilton qualified ahead of both Raikkonen and Alonso only to lose out to them at the start. Worse still, he fell to eighth after making a hash of an attempted pass on Alonso. A gearbox glitch then dropped him further down the field. It cleared, but he was able to recover to no higher than seventh.

All Raikkonen had to do now was win the race, and he duly did so, passing a co-operative Massa at the second pit stop to take the race lead and go on to win the championship by a single point.

2008

On which lap of the Singapore Grand Prix did Nelson Piquet Jr. infamously crash out of the race?

B.   Fourteen

It's not easy to pass at Singapore. Not easy at all.

So when Fernando Alonso qualified 15th there can't have been too many people who expected him to stand on the top step of the podium come the end of the race. And yet that's what happened.

Alonso's car had been short-fuelled, meaning that he'd have make an early pit-stop. He was therefore the first car to stop, on lap 12, dropping him to last place. That was, however, about to change.

On lap 14, Alonso's team-mate, Nelson Piquet Jr., contrived to crash out of the race at a point of the circuit from which his car could not easily be recovered. Cue a Safety Car and a mad scramble for the pits. Chaos ensued as most of the field pitted to take on fuel and fresh tyres. The races of several drivers were ruined through having to double-stack, but Felipe Massa was worst affected: an error with his pit 'traffic light' system meant that he was released while the fuel hose was still attached to his Ferrari. Massa had been leading the race when the Safety Car was deployed but the effects of the incident saw him finish out of the points.

Alonso emerged from the chaos in fifth place, but the four cars running ahead of him had yet to make their pit stops. One by one, they peeled off to take on fuel and fresh tyres, the result being that Alonso found himself leading the race. And with passing being so difficult at Singapore, he was able to maintain that lead to the chequered flag.

There was speculation at the time that there was more than met the eye to Piquet's crash, but it wasn't until nearly a year later that Brazilian media opened a veritable can of worms by reporting that Piquet had allegedly crashed in compliance with instructions given to him.

Piquet had in fact already given a statement to the FIA to that effect. 'Crashgate', as it became known, thereafter played out in both the courts and the media for many months thereafter.

2009

Who partnered Kimi Raikkonen at Ferrari for the last five Grands Prix of the season?

A.   Giancarlo Fisichella

After Felipe Massa was injured in qualifying for the Hungarian Grand Prix, it soon became evident that he would not be able to return to Formula One that season.

Ferrari initially sought to replace him with test driver Luca Badoer. But after ten years away from racing, it was a tall order to expect Badoer to be on the pace. Too tall: he qualified 20th and last at both Valencia and Spa and his race pace was no better.

The Scuderia therefore turned to Giancarlo Fisichella, then driving for Force India. It was a decision that seemed to make sense: Fisichella was an experienced and able driver who was in good form, having taken pole position at Spa and followed that up with second place in the race.

Unfortunately, that season's Ferrari, the F60, was not one of the Scuderia's better efforts. Fisichella was unable to match Raikkonen's pace in the sister car, failing to score a single world championship point in five races. He remained with Ferrari for 2010 as reserve driver but never again raced in Formula One.

2010 – 2020

2010

Red Bull team-mates Vettel and Webber collided when disputing the lead of which Grand Prix?

B.   Turkey

It's probably fair to say that Mark Webber and Sebastian Vettel didn't always enjoy the most harmonious of relationships at Red Bull.

For example, there was the 'Multi-21' affair at the 2013 Malaysian Grand Prix, when Vettel ignored team instructions to hold station behind Webber. There was also the saga of the front wing at Silverstone in 2010, when Webber's new specification front wing was given to his team-mate after the German damaged the one he had been allocated. An unamused Webber went on to win the race, his "Not bad for a Number Two driver" comment on team radio becoming part of F1 lore.

But before either of those events came the 2010 Turkish Grand Prix. Webber led from pole, with Vettel jumping Hamilton for second at the pit stops. Now the two Red Bulls led from the two McLarens. It was a narrow lead, however, with Hamilton bringing increasing pressure to bear on Vettel.

On lap 40, Vettel got a run on Webber down the straight leading to turn 12. He got his nose ahead of his team-mate and started to pull over to the right. But with Webber having held his line, the two made contact, Vettel's right rear tyre striking the left-hand endplate of Webber's front wing.

The collision caused both Red Bulls to leave the track, Webber going straight on at turn 12 whilst Vettel, his tyre punctured, spun out of the race. The McLarens of Hamilton and Button gleefully accepted the gift and went on to finish first and second, with a furious Webber coming home third after a stop for a new nosecone.

2011

Who finished second to Sebastian Vettel in the Drivers' Championship?

D.   Jenson Button

Beating Lewis Hamilton in an equal car over the course of a Formula One season is a tough proposition. But Jenson Button, Hamilton's team-mate at McLaren from 2010 to 2012, did just that.

In some ways, the Button - Hamilton partnership resembled that of Prost and Senna, with Button not always being as quick as Hamilton but more than capable of putting together a highly impressive series of results.

Indeed, over the course of the three seasons that they raced together, Button took 8 wins to Hamilton's 10 but outscored him in terms of both podiums and points.

Button's best year in that regard was 2011, when his points tally of 270 meant that he finished in second place in the world championship, some 43 points and three places ahead of Hamilton.

2012

In which Grand Prix did Michael Schumacher score his 155th and last podium finish?

D.   Europe (Valencia)

Michael Schumacher's F1 career from 2010 to 2012 stands in stark contrast to that from 1991 to 2006.

When he retired, temporarily as it happened, in 2006, the older of the Schumacher brothers had scored 91 victories and a further 63 podiums in only 250 Grands Prix, a remarkable achievement by any yardstick. But in the 58 Grands Prix he contested for Mercedes between 2010 and the end of the 2012 season, he took but one podium – a third place in the 2012

European Grand Prix at Valencia.

2013

For which team did Charles Pic drive in 2013?

A.   Caterham

A multiple race winner in both Formula Renault 3.5 and GP2, Charles Pic raced in 39 Grands Prix over two seasons.

He drove alongside Timo Glock for Marussia in 2012, mostly losing out to his more experienced team-mate in qualifying and ending the season with a best race finish of 15th.

Pic moved to Caterham for 2013 and matched new team-mate Giedo van der Garde for pace, but neither he nor van der Garde was able to finish a Grand Prix in a points paying position.

Unable to find a race seat for 2014, Pic became the reserve driver for Lotus F1, but his relationship with the team ended in a legal dispute. He returned to racing in September 2014 and contested five rounds of the inaugural Formula E championship.

It was a short-lived return, as in 2015 he accepted a management position with a French logistics company, for whom he continues to work.

2014

In what place did Sebastian Vettel finish in the 2014 world championship?

B.   Fifth

Having won four World Drivers' Championships on the trot, Sebastian Vettel's chances of adding a fifth title in 2014 were undone by a radical change in the engine regulations.

Gone were the normally aspirated V8 engines which had powered his Red Bull to all four championships and in came turbocharged 1.6 litre hybrid power units. With a clean slate from which to work, it was Mercedes, not Renault, who produced the best of the new engines.

The Mercedes hybrid engine was powerful, flexible, fuel-efficient, reliable and was mated to a fine chassis. Add in the driving skills of Lewis Hamilton and Nico Rosberg and Mercedes had everything they required in order to dominate the 2014 F1 season. And that's just what they did.

Vettel may not have had the best car that season, but even so his performance was curiously off-key. He failed to win a single Grand Prix and was eclipsed in the standings by not only the Mercedes duo but also by his new teammate, Daniel Ricciardo, who won three times that season, and Williams's Valtteri Bottas.

2015

Where did McLaren finish in the 2015 Constructors' standings?

D.   Ninth

Having enjoyed more than a decade of success with Mercedes engines, McLaren took the bold decision to switch to Honda power for 2015, thereby reviving their fruitful partnership of the late 1980s and early 1990s.

It was, alas, to be a different story this time, with the Woking team (and Fernando Alonso, in particular) struggling to cope with the inevitable growing pains of the Honda powerplant.

Performance and reliability were both poor, with former world champions Alonso and Button recording only two finishes in the top six all year. This was reflected in the team's lowly ninth place finish in the Constructors' Championship, their final tally of 27 points being 154 fewer than they had amassed in 2014.

Although matters improved somewhat in 2016, with the team scoring 76 points and finishing sixth in the Constructors' Championship, a very poor 2017 (30 points and ninth in the table) marked the end of the McLaren-Honda relationship, with the Woking team moving to Renault power for 2018.

As for Honda, they forged a new partnership with Red Bull Racing, winning three Grands Prix and finishing third in the Constructors' Championship in 2019.

2016

Who replaced Rio Haryanto at Manor from the Belgian Grand Prix onwards?

A.   Esteban Ocon

Having finished fourth in the 2015 GP2 championship, Rio Haryanto became the first Indonesian driver to race in Formula One when he started the 2016 Australian Grand Prix.

Haryanto would not, however, see out the season, being demoted to reserve driver after the German Grand Prix. He was replaced by Mercedes protégé Esteban Ocon, whose performances relative to team-mate Pascal Wehrlein were broadly on a par with those of Haryanto.

After Manor folded at the end of season, Wehrlein and Ocon both continued in F1 with other teams, but Haryanto was left without a drive. Indeed, his only full-time race seat since then has been in the Blancpain GT World Challenge Asia series in 2019.

2017

Which driver won the 'Breakthrough of the year' award (for achievements in 2016) at the Laureus Sports Awards?

C.   Nico Rosberg

The by-now retired Nico Rosberg won the Breakthrough award, in spite of having raced in F1 for ten full seasons and having won 14 Grands Prix prior to his 2016 world championship season.

The decision to award Rosberg the Breakthrough prize is all the more curious when one considers that Max Verstappen, then aged 18, had not only won his first Grand Prix for Red Bull but had become the youngest-ever driver to win a Grand Prix in so doing. As it was, however, Verstappen wasn't even among the nominees for the award.

2018

In which race was the chequered flag mistakenly shown a lap too soon?

C.   Canada

Model Winnie Harlow had been invited to show the chequered flag to end the Grand Prix. Unfortunately, a misunderstanding between race officials meant that she was asked to wave it at the end of lap 69, a lap too early.

Race leader Sebastian Vettel noticed the error and, thinking that it would be corrected, continued at unabated pace until he had completed the full 70 laps.

Under the regulations, however, the race result was declared on the basis of the race positions as at lap 68. This did not affect the points-scoring positions but meant that the fastest race laps set by Daniel Ricciardo on laps 69 and 70 did not count, with the result that his Red Bull team-mate Max Verstappen was awarded fastest lap.

As an extra point for fastest lap in a Grand Prix was not awarded in 2018, this made no difference to the points tally of either driver.

2019

At which Grand Prix did Charles Leclerc take his first pole position in Formula One?

B.   Bahrain

Leclerc showed impressive qualifying speed in his first season with Ferrari, taking pole position at seven* of the twenty-one Grands Prix, the most of any driver on the grid.

Although his race pace generally failed to match his qualifying speed and his driving was sometimes a little erratic, he nonetheless outscored his illustrious team-mate Sebastian Vettel both in terms of points scored and races won.

* This includes the Mexican Grand Prix, in which he was second fastest in qualifying but started from pole following the imposition of a three place grid penalty on Max Verstappen.

2020

What does the acronym DAS stand for on the Mercedes W11?

B.   Dual Axis Steering

Mercedes surprised everyone in winter testing for the 2020 world championship by outfitting their cars with a system that allows the alignment (known as the 'toe') of their car's front wheels to be adjusted via the steering wheel.

On F1 cars the front tyres will usually appear to point slightly away from each other. This set-up is known as toe-out and is used to help cars turn in to corners a little more eagerly. There is, however, a small price to pay for this in terms of aerodynamic efficiency and tyre wear.

The DAS system designed by Mercedes allows the drivers to dynamically adjust their car's toe, so that the front tyres point in a straight line down the straights but also have the benefit of toe-out when cornering. The benefits in terms of improved aerodynamics and lower tyre wear are unlikely to be substantial, but Formula One is very much a game of small margins.

But with the FIA having decreed that DAS will be outlawed as from the 2021 season, its impact will be short-lived.

General Knowledge I

G1

Which country has hosted the most Grands Prix?

C.   Italy

In addition to the Italian Grand Prix, held every year since 1950, Italy has also played host to the San Marino Grand Prix on 26 occasions, plus the 1957 Pescara Grand Prix, thus making a total of 97 Grands Prix held on Italian soil as at the end of the 2019 season.

In spite of not having hosted a Grand Prix in every year of Formula One's existence (only Britain and Italy have done so), Germany is next up, having hosted a total of 78 Grands Prix - 64 German, 12 European and 2 Luxembourg Grands Prix.

G2

Who did Michael Schumacher replace at Jordan when he made his F1 debut?

D.   Bertrand Gachot

Gachot lost his seat at Jordan for a very unusual reason – he was in a British jail!

Several months previously, the Belgian driver had got involved in an altercation with a London taxi driver, in the course of which he sprayed the cabbie with CS gas. Unbeknown to him, it was illegal to possess CS gas in the UK, let alone use it. And so, just a matter of days after setting fastest lap in the 1991 Hungarian Grand Prix, Gachot found himself being sentenced to six months in prison.

With Gachot behind bars, Eddie Jordan found himself in need of a replacement driver for the Belgian Grand Prix. Cue the arrival in F1 of Michael Schumacher, who made a big first impression by qualifying a superb 7th.

As for Gachot, he was subsequently released on appeal. Two months had passed, however, during which time his place at Jordan had been taken by a succession of other drivers, of whom Schumacher was the first. Gachot did, however, return to F1 with the Larrousse and, later, Pacific teams.

His F1 career came to a halt at the end of the 1995 season and he thereafter began to focus more on a career in business.

G3

In what year did the six-wheel Tyrrell P34 make its debut?

B.   1976

Designed by Derek Gardner, the Tyrrell P34 featured four small front wheels rather than two large ones.

The rationale behind this revolutionary idea was that the use of smaller front wheels would reduce the amount of drag and also tidy up the airflow to the rear wing. It wasn't, however, an unequivocal success, and driver Jody Scheckter was typically forthright in his description of its flaws.

The P34 particularly struggled on bumpier circuits, so it's perhaps no surprise that its sole Grand Prix victory came in the 1976 Swedish Grand Prix on the smooth surface of the Anderstorp circuit. Indeed, the Tyrrells came in first and second that day.

The P34 thereafter soldiered on for another season, but results were very hard to come by in 1977. Its weight had increased and the unique 10 inch tyres that were fitted to its front wheels suffered from a lack of development.

Several other six-wheel F1 cars were built and tested by Ferrari, Williams and March. None of these designs shared the P34's arrangement of four wheels at the front and two at the rear, however, nor did any of them ever race in a Grand Prix.

G4

Who is the only driver to have won the world championship with both Ferrari and McLaren?

B.   Niki Lauda

Lauda won the championship twice for Ferrari (in 1975 and 1977), went to Brabham, retired, returned for McLaren and, in 1984, won the title again.

Prost and Raikkonen both came close to emulating his feat. Prost won three championships with McLaren and was runner-up for Ferrari in 1990. Raikkonen did it the other way around, twice finishing runner-up in the standings for McLaren but winning the title in 2007 for Ferrari.

Senna won all three of his world championships for McLaren but never raced for Ferrari in F1.

G5

Who replaced Alain Prost at Ferrari for the final Grand Prix in 1991?

D.   Gianni Morbidelli

Alain Prost had a torrid 1991 season due to Ferrari's failure to consolidate the gains they had made in 1990.

Neither the 642 that had shown so well the previous season nor the new 643, which was introduced at the French Grand Prix, were on a par with their main rivals, the Williams FW14 and the McLaren MP4/6. The result: a winless season for the Scuderia.

Prost's frustration eventually boiled over, resulting in him comparing his Ferrari to a truck after his power steering failed at Suzuka, an outburst that symptomised deeper tensions in his relationship with the Scuderia. Accordingly, his sacking by Ferrari prior to the season-ending Australian Grand Prix came as no great shock.

Prost was replaced for that race by Gianni Morbidelli, a young Italian driver who had been racing in F1 for Minardi. Morbidelli did well enough on his sole Ferrari outing, qualifying 8th and finishing sixth in a race that was stopped after 14 of the scheduled 81 laps after a number of cars had crashed in appalling weather conditions.

It was Morbidelli's one and only chance to drive for a top team, although he did go on to compete in a total of 70 Grands Prix and score a podium for Footwork in 1994.

G6

What team won Grands Prix in 1982 with two different engines?

A.   Brabham

Even the most imaginative Hollywood screenwriter would struggle to come up with a script that could match the 1982 F1 season for sheer drama.

It started out with a driver's strike prior to the season-opening South African Grand Prix, which resulted in the drivers sleeping on the floor of a hotel conference room.

That issue was no sooner sorted out than the cars that finished first and second in the Brazilian Grand Prix were both disqualified, leading to further unrest between the sport's governing body and most of the teams. This in turn led to a boycott of the San Marino Grand Prix by the likes of Williams, McLaren and Ligier. Tragedy followed in both Belgium and Canada, with Gilles Villeneuve and Ricardo Paletti perishing.

Between times there was high comedy in Monaco, where car after car led the race in the closing stages only to lose it for a variety of different reasons; innovation in Britain, where the Brabham team introduced mid-race fuel stops; drama in Germany, where Nelson Piquet assaulted a backmarker who tripped him up; a surprise win in Austria for Lotus (their first victory in four years and the last during founder Colin Chapman's lifetime); and emotion in Monza, where forty-two year old Mario Andretti returned to the Ferrari team a decade after last racing for them in F1, taking pole position and finishing third in the race.

There was also a record number of race winners: eleven drivers and seven teams. No driver won more than two Grands Prix, and the champion, Finland's Keke Rosberg, took but a single victory.

Oh, and Patrese won at Monaco in a Ford-powered Brabham, with team-mate Piquet using a turbocharged BMW engine to take victory in Canada.

You really couldn't make it up.

G7

In what season did a stray priest result in a Safety Car at the British Grand Prix?

A.   2003

For the second time in three years (the 2000 German Grand Prix was the first), a Grand Prix was interrupted because of the presence of a spectator on the track.

Having climbed over the safety fencing, the invader, a middle-aged man wearing an orange skirt and carrying a banner exhorting people to read the Bible, ran down Hangar Straight towards the Becketts complex and into the path of oncoming cars. Thankfully, disaster was averted due to the quick reactions of drivers and marshals alike.

The intruder, a Roman Catholic priest named Neil Horan, was subsequently convicted of aggravated trespass and sentenced to two months' imprisonment.

Sadly, he did not learn his lesson. At the 2004 Olympic Games in Athens, Horan interfered with the Men's Marathon by running onto the course at about the 35 kilometre mark and pushing the race leader, Vanderlei de Lima, into the crowd. Although de Lima was able to continue, Horan's actions cost him much of the lead he had built up, and he eventually finished third.

Horan escaped imprisonment that time round but was subsequently removed from the clergy.

G8

How many drivers have retired from F1 immediately after winning the world championship?

B.   Four

Having won the world championship in 1958, Mike Hawthorn kept a promise he had made to himself earlier that year and immediately retired from motor racing. Hawthorn's decision was most likely due to two factors: the death of his close friend Peter Collins in that year's German Grand Prix and the effects of a chronic, and probably life-shortening, kidney condition which had affected him for a number of years.

Tragically, Hawthorn did not live long to enjoy his achievement of having become the first Briton to win the world championship. He was killed in a road accident on the Guildford Bypass three months after his final Grand. He was just 29 years of age.

Jackie Stewart's retirement after winning his third world championship in 1973 was also tinged with tragedy. Stewart had decided earlier that year that he would retire but had told very few people of his decision. Indeed, he hadn't even told his wife, not wanting her to mentally start counting down the races until his last, lest fate have other plans for him.

Stewart was very close to his team-mate, Francois Cevert. Having befriended and mentored Cevert, Stewart had come to think of him almost as a younger brother. Cevert knew nothing, however, of Stewart's plans, nor did he know that he would be taking Stewart's place as the lead driver for the Tyrrell team in 1974.

The final race of the season, the United States Grand Prix at Watkins Glen, would have been Stewart's 100th Grand Prix had tragedy not struck in qualifying.

Cevert's Tyrrell got out of shape when he was attempting to improve on his lap time by taking the sequence of corners known as *"the Esses"* in third gear rather than fourth. His car clipped a kerb before striking crash barriers on the right hand side of the track. The angle and speed of the impact then threw it across the track and into another crash barrier, which it struck head-on, causing it to lift. The accident was unsurvivable.

Understandably, neither Stewart nor Chris Amon, who was driving a third Tyrrell that weekend, took part in the race.

Alain Prost, a driver whose highly intelligent approach to racing was reminiscent of Jackie Stewart, was the next defending champion to walk away from F1, never to return as a driver.

Having won three world championships, Prost found himself without a race seat for 1992 after being dismissed by Ferrari. He returned in 1993 with Williams and strolled to his fourth world championship without ever quite reaching the heights he had once ascended. He might have stayed to defend his title in 1994 but for the Williams team's decision to sign Ayrton Senna.

With no appetite for a repeat of the clashes he had experienced with Senna during the latter part of their time as team-mates at McLaren, Prost decided to bow out from F1 at the top.

It's pertinent, I think, to add that in the few months that followed, Senna reached out to Prost. His overtures were well received by Prost, and a rapprochement that few could have envisaged started to take shape. Indeed, Prost believes that the two could well have gone on to enjoy a good friendship had Senna not perished at Imola in 1994.

The last of the four reigning world champions to permanently retire from F1 is, of course, Nico Rosberg. Having won the championship in 2016, after battling long and hard with Lewis Hamilton for four seasons, Rosberg decided that he had neither the need nor desire to fight another campaign.

I've not included Nigel Mansell, the 1992 world champion, in this list, as although he said he was retiring from F1 after failing to reach agreement with Williams for 1993, this announcement turned out to be somewhat premature. He returned to F1 in 1994 and drove in four Grands Prix for William, winning one of them.

Mansell thereafter signed a multi-year contract to race in F1 for McLaren, albeit his stay with the Woking-based team turned out to be a short one.

G9

Where did Michael Schumacher notch his first Grand Prix victory?

B.   Spa-Francorchamps

One year on from his F1 debut at the Ardennes Circuit, Michael Schumacher took his first Grand Prix win in a race held in changeable conditions.

As was his wont that season, Mansell led the way for much of the race, seemingly heading for yet another victory. The trajectory of the race changed, however, when Schumacher, then running in third position, had a minor off-track excursion on lap 30 that lost him a place to his team-mate, Martin Brundle.

As he followed Brundle, Schumacher noted that the wet tyres on the Englishman's car were blistering. Accordingly, he decided to stop and change his own wet tyres for a set of slicks. It was the right decision, and Schumacher was soon lapping fastest of all the remaining runners.

Williams were a little slow in reacting, with the result that Schumacher passed Mansell for the lead when the latter pitted. Had Mansell's car stayed healthy, it's likely that he'd have caught the young German and re-taken the lead. However, a misfire ended his charge and allowed Schumacher to coast home for his first Grand Prix victory.

G10

How many drivers have won both the F1 world championship and the Indianapolis 500?

B.   Five

Jim Clark was the first driver to complete the double by winning at Indianapolis in 1965.

He also won the F1 world championship again that year, thus making him the only driver have won the world championship and the Indy 500 in the same season – a record that still stands.

Clark's great friend and rival, Graham Hill, won at Indianapolis the following year, thus adding it to the world championship he had won in 1962.

A dozen years then passed before Mario Andretti completed the double by adding the F1 world championship to his 1969 Indianapolis 500 victory, and a further eleven years would go by before double F1 world champion Emerson Fittipaldi added the first of his two Indianapolis 500 wins to his CV.

Most recently, Jacques Villeneuve added his name to the list, winning at Indy in 1995 and taking the world championship in 1997. Since then, only Fernando Alonso has attempted to join the club, having led the Indianapolis 500 in 2017.

General Knowledge II

G11

How many Grands Prix were won by cars powered by BRM's V12 engine?

B.   Four

BRM-powered cars competed in Formula One from 1951 to 1977, taking eighteen Grand Prix victories between 1959 and 1972 using four different engine configurations: straight four, V8, V12 and H16.

With twelve Grand Prix wins between 1962 and 1966, the V8 was BRM's most successful engine. A change in the engine regulations saw it phased out in 1966 in favour of a new 3.0 litre H16 engine that emphatically failed to match its predecessor's success.

BRM introduced another new engine, a V12, in 1967. This unit was initially used only by the McLaren team, but BRM themselves used it from 1968 onwards. It powered the Bourne team's cars to four Grand Prix wins and remained their frontline engine until they left the world championship at the end of the 1977 season.

G12

What was Swedish driver Tommy 'Slim' Borgudd's other job?

C.   Session drummer who had worked with Abba

Slim Borgudd's talent behind a drum kit was matched by his ability at the wheel of a racing car.

His love of both music and motorsport was reflected in his career choices, and he performed with a number of bands in his native Sweden whilst attempting to forge a career as a racing driver.

Like most racers, then and now, Borgudd struggled to raise the funding he needed in order to compete. He persevered, however, and finally got his shot at F1 in 1981 with the ATS team.

The ATS was far from being the class of the field, but the large ABBA decals that it carried on its sidepods certainly made it stand out. With seventeen teams competing for much of the season, competition was fierce in 1981. Borgudd did fairly well, though, and scored a world championship point for taking sixth place in the British Grand Prix.

He left ATS at the end of the season and started the following season at Tyrrell but left the team – and F1 - when his sponsorship funds ran out.

At 35, his brief F1 career was over, though he continued to race in other formulae until finally retiring in 1997.

G13

For which team did 1976 world champion James Hunt last race in F1?

D.   Wolf

James Hunt left McLaren at the end of 1978 to join the Wolf team.

According to Wolf team manager, Peter Warr, Hunt's heart wasn't in it from the outset, and it came as no great surprise when he announced his retirement after the 1979 Monaco Grand Prix.

The Wolf team continued until the end of the season, with Keke Rosberg having replaced Hunt. It was then sold to the Fittipaldi team, for whom Rosberg went on to drive in 1980.

In that same year, 1980, McLaren asked Hunt to drive for them as a stand-in for the injured Alain Prost. He might well have done so had he not broken a leg on a skiing holiday. As it was, another British driver, Stephen South, stood in for Prost at the US (West) Grand Prix at Long Beach.

Rumours of a comeback continued to do the rounds over the years, and Hunt (at age 43) tested a Williams in 1989. Nothing came of either the rumours or the test, however, and Hunt never returned to F1.

G14

What was the type number of the Lotus F1 car that made its debut in 1969?

B.   Type 63

Introduced in 1967, the Lotus 49 continued to serve the team, in updated form, until being replaced by the Type 72 in 1970.

The 49 was not, however, the only Lotus F1 car to take to the track in 1969, for it was accompanied by a new, all-wheel-drive car, the Type 63.

The 63 differed from the 49 in two significant ways: it had wedge-shaped bodywork and all-wheel-drive, both derived from the Type 56 that raced in the 1968 Indianapolis 500.

Whilst a great idea in theory, the four-wheel drive system added weight and made the 63 difficult to set up. Worst of all, it was slow.

Lotus persevered with it, perhaps buoyed by Jochen Rindt's second place finish in the non-championship Oulton Park Gold Cup. Even so, neither Hill nor Rindt ever raced it in a Grand Prix, that thankless task being left to John Miles and Mario Andretti. It failed to finish all but one of the seven Grands Prix it contested. Its one and only finish came in Germany, where Miles took it to tenth place.

It was quietly shelved at the end of the season. It wasn't, however, the last four-wheel-drive Lotus to contest a Grand Prix – the Type 56 was dusted down, reworked into the Type 56B and used sparingly in the 1971 F1 season.

G15

Which driver holds the record for the longest time between Grand Prix wins?

B.   Riccardo Patrese

Over six and a half years (October 1983 to May 1990) elapsed between Riccardo Patrese's second and third Grand Prix wins. He thereafter won another three Grands Prix in the following two seasons.

Of the others in the list, both Rubens Barrichello and John Watson went four years and 11 months between victories, while Kimi Raikkonen endured a fallow period of five years and seven months.

Looked at in terms of the number of races contested between Grand Prix victories, it is Kimi Raikkonen who holds the record, he having raced in 113 Grands Prix between his wins at Australia in 2013 and the USA in 2018.

Raikkonen also currently holds the record for the time elapsed between his first and last (to date) Grand Prix victories, the two being separated by 15 years and 212 days.

G16

Who has won all 3 Indian Grands Prix to date?

A.   Sebastian Vettel

The Indian Grand Prix was hosted by the Buddh International Circuit from 2011 to 2013.

It disappeared from the calendar for 2014 due to a dispute over taxes between the organisers and the government for the region in which the track is situated. Although it was originally scheduled to return in 2015, it has never reappeared on the F1 calendar.

That leaves Sebastian Vettel as the only driver ever to have won the Indian Grand Prix, he having triumphed in 2011, 2012 and 2013.

G17

For which team did Damon Hill drive in 1997?

D.   Arrows

For the third time in the 1990s, a driver who won the world championship in a Williams did not remain with the team to defend his title.

In Hill's case, the team had decided not to renew his contract at the end of the 1996 season, having signed Heinz-Harald Frentzen as a replacement. Hill therefore drove the final part of the 1996 season in the knowledge that he would have to find a drive with another team for 1997 irrespective of whether or not he won the world championship.

He held talks with both Ferrari and McLaren but ended up at Arrows – a team that had been in the sport for nearly two decades without winning a Grand Prix. Hill came agonisingly close to changing that, leading the Hungarian Grand Prix with ease until a late-race hydraulic problem cost him several seconds a lap and enabled Jacques Villeneuve, his former Williams team-mate, to pass him on the final tour.

Hill would, however, win again in F1, taking the Jordan team's first win in a wet/dry race at Spa in 1998. He retired at the end of the following season.

G18

What is the only circuit on the F1 calendar to use a figure of 8 layout?

D.   Suzuka

When Suzuka first hosted the Japanese Grand Prix in 1987, it was the first time since Monza in 1961 that a Grand Prix had been run on a circuit with a figure of 8 layout.

Although Suzuka's figure of 8 layout is an integral part of the full circuit (the bridge on the exit of the second *Degner* corner marks the point where the track crosses over itself), Monza's figure of 8 layout used a combination of the road circuit and a banked oval circuit that crossed over the road circuit on the run down the to the *Variante Ascari*.

Although last used for a Grand Prix in 1961, Monza's banked circuit featured in the 1966 movie, *Grand Prix*. It still exists today, albeit it is no longer used for racing.

As of May, 2020, the Fiorano circuit in Italy is the only other FIA Grade 1 circuit (and, as such, licensed to host a Grand Prix) to have a figure of 8 layout.

G19

Who was the only driver to race in F1 for both Matra teams?

B.　　Jean-Pierre Beltoise

Having diversified into sports car manufacture in 1964, it made sense for French aerospace and defence company Matra to move into motorsport.

They took to it like the proverbial duck to water, winning in both Formula 3 and Formula 2 before taking the plunge into F1 in 1968. Unusually, though, they entered the championship as two teams – the full works Matra Sports outfit, which would use the company's brand new V12 engine, and the semi-works Matra International team, run by Ken Tyrrell and using Matra chassis powered by the Ford Cosworth DFV V8.

Beltoise contested the first two Grands Prix for Matra International, moving to Matra Sports once the V12-powered MS11 car was ready. Of the other three men who drove for Matra in F1 that season, two (Jackie Stewart and Johnny Servoz-Gavin) drove solely for Matra International and the other, Henri Pescarolo, drove only for Matra Sports.

Stewart had a strong 1968 season in the Ford-powered MS10, winning three Grands Prix in spite of having to sit out two races due to a broken wrist. The Matra-powered MS11 found the going a little tougher, however, although Beltoise memorably drove it to second place, behind Stewart in the MS10, in the Dutch Grand Prix.

The success of Matra International and the need to continue development work on their V12 engine resulted in Matra deciding to put all their eggs in the Matra International basket for 1969, the drivers being Stewart and Beltoise. The result: Stewart won his first World Drivers' Championship and Matra International won the Constructors' Cup.

G20

Chris Amon drove for how many different constructors in Formula One?

A.   Thirteen

Chris Amon was a hugely gifted driver who experienced perennial bad luck in F1. Indeed, Mario Andretti once quipped that if Amon became an undertaker, people would stop dying!

It seems appropriate, therefore, that he drove thirteen different makes of car in Grands Prix: Lola, Lotus, BRM, Brabham, Cooper, Ferrari, March, Matra, Tecno, Tyrrell, Amon, Ensign, and Wolf-Williams – a tally that remains a record to this day.

The misfortune that befell Amon in Grands Prix did not, however, extend to non-championship F1 races (of which he won two) and other forms of motorsport – his triumphs included the 1966 Le Mans 24 Hours, the 1967 Daytona 24 Hours and the 1969 Tasman Series.

Amon took a sanguine view of his misfortunes as a Grand Prix driver, however, noting that he had been fortunate enough to survive the sport's deadliest era whilst many of his friends and contemporaries had not.

General Knowledge III

G21

Which of the following British drivers did NOT drive for Team Lotus in a Grand Prix?

B.   Tony Trimmer.

Although Tony Trimmer drove for Team Lotus in three non-championship events in 1971, starting two of them, he never raced for them in a Grand Prix.

Of Trimmer's six attempts to qualify for a Grand Prix, four were made for the Japanese Maki team and the other two for Melchester Racing. Unfortunately, he was unsuccessful in all of those attempts.

Watson, Henton and Crawford started a total of five Grands Prix between them for Team Lotus in 1975. The team's fortunes were, however, at a low point at that time, and their combined efforts failed to yield a single championship point.

G22

Who is the last defending F1 world champion not to have won a Grand Prix in the season following his title win?

D.   Sebastian Vettel

Vettel had been utterly dominant in 2013, winning thirteen Grands Prix, but was unable to muster even a single victory in defence of his title, and that in a year when his much less experienced team-mate took three wins.

Vettel is far from the only defending champion to fail to win a Grand Prix in defence of his title. He is joined in that regard by Damon Hill, Jacques Villeneuve, Mario Andretti, Jody Scheckter, Jack Brabham, Phil Hill, John Surtees and Nelson Piquet. Alberto Ascari, champion in 1952 and 1953, failed to win a Grand Prix in 1954 but only contested four Grands Prix that season. Likewise, Juan Manuel Fangio, champion from 1954 to 1957, only drove in two Grands Prix in 1958.

G23

Who was the youngest driver to start a Grand Prix in 2019?

B.   Lando Norris

With an average age of 26 years and 3 months when the season began in Melbourne, the 2019 Formula One grid was the youngest ever.

The youngest driver in Melbourne was McLaren's Lando Norris, born in November 1999. In terms of youth, he was followed by Lance Stroll, born in October 1998, and George Russell, born in February 1998.

In comparison, Pierre Gasly is something of a senior citizen, having been born in February 1996. Indeed, Gasly is also older than Max Verstappen (September 1997), Charles Leclerc (October 1997) and Alexander Albon (March 1996).

G24

What new career did Jaime Alguersuari forge after retiring from motorsport at the age of 25?

C.   Disc jockey

When he made his F1 debut for Toro Rosso at the 2009 Hungarian Grand Prix, Alguersuari became the youngest ever driver to start a Grand Prix, a record since taken by Max Verstappen.

Alguersuari remained with Toro Rosso until the end of the 2011 season, after which he became the test driver for Pirelli's F1 tyre programme. He thereafter drove for Virgin Racing in Formula E before deciding to retire from motorsport and concentrate on his burgeoning career as a DJ.

G25

Who raced for Ferrari in the 1952 Indianapolis 500?

B.   Alberto Ascari

Alberto Ascari was the man chosen to lead Ferrari's assault on the 1952 Indianapolis 500.

The Scuderia had intended to enter two suitably modified Ferrari 375s for Ascari and Nino Farina, but that plan had to be shelved after Farina crashed his 375 in a race in Turin. Another three 375s were entered by private teams based in the USA, but none of them made the race, leaving Ascari as the sole Ferrari representative.

Having qualified 25th, he worked his way up through the field and was running just outside the top 10 when a seized wheel bearing caused him to spin out of the race.

It would be 48 years before Ferrari returned to Indianapolis, but this time it would be for the US Grand Prix rather than the '500'.

G26

How many Grands Prix did Lewis Hamilton win at McLaren?

D.   Twenty-one

In the six seasons that he raced for McLaren, Lewis Hamilton won a total of twenty-one Grands Prix.

He took four victories in 2007, his debut season, and notched a further five wins on his way to the 2008 World Drivers' Championship. He won a further twelve Grands Prix in the next four seasons, but things were a little tougher in terms of championship success, with two fourth places being his best finishes in the points standings prior to his 2013 move to Mercedes.

He took just one Grand Prix victory in that first season with Mercedes, but the change in the engine formula that took effect in 2014 saw a dramatic upturn in fortune for both team and driver, for in the six full seasons since the hybrid engines were introduced Hamilton has won sixty-two Grands Prix.

G27

By what other surname was Ayrton Senna known?

A.   da Silva

Under Portuguese and Spanish naming customs, people typically have two family names. The first of these is the surname of their mother, and the second is the surname of their father.

When he first came to the UK, Ayrton Senna da Silva originally raced as 'Ayrton da Silva'. In 1982, however, he decided to race under his mother's surname instead. His reason for doing this was to give himself a more distinctive identity from a sporting and sponsorship perspective, 'da Silva' being the most common surname in Brazil.

There was nothing remarkable about Senna's decision. Indeed, it's not uncommon for drivers from Spanish or Portuguese-speaking countries to use their maternal surname. For example, Nelson Piquet's full name is Nelson Piquet Soutomaior. He started using his mother's surname after taking up karting, as he didn't want his father to find out that he'd started racing. And in more recent times, Fernando Alonso Diaz has achieved worldwide fame as Fernando Alonso.

G28

Who scored the last Grand Prix win for a front-engined car?

D.   Phil Hill

The record books show that Phil Hill took Ferrari's only Grand Prix win of 1960 (and the last for a front-engined F1 car) at the Italian Grand Prix.

What the records fail to mention is that the race, run on the combined road and banked circuit at Monza, was boycotted by Cooper, BRM and Lotus on safety grounds. This left the Ferrari team, which had hitherto been also-rans that season, to take a clean sweep of the podium positions.

Hill's victory is also noteworthy for another reason: it was the first Grand Prix win by a driver from the USA.

G29

Which of the following drivers has NOT raced for Sauber in a Grand Prix?

C.   Sergey Sirotkin

Sirotkin was the Sauber team's test driver from July 2013 to the end of the 2014 season. He drove for the team in free practice at the 2014 Russian Grand Prix but never raced in a Grand Prix.

He had a similar role with Renault in 2016 and 2017 before finally gaining a race seat with Williams for the 2018 season. As of 2020, he is the reserve driver for the Renault F1 team.

G30

For which team did Niki Lauda first race in F1?

A.   March

If you've seen the film 'Rush' and think that Lauda's first F1 drive was with BRM then think again!

Lauda made his F1 debut at the 1971 Austrian Grand Prix in a one-off drive for the March team. He thereafter joined March on a full-time basis for the 1972 season, partnering rising Swedish star, Ronnie Peterson. Unfortunately for Lauda, March had a somewhat trying 1972 season, in which they ran three different cars: the 721, the experimental (and very unsuccessful) 721X and the hastily put together 721G.

Lauda failed to score a point that season, and even Peterson (runner-up to Jackie Stewart in the 1971 world championship) was only able to score 12 points.

The Austrian moved to BRM for 1973, but the team was in decline and he managed to score only two points that season. However, his BRM team-mate Clay Regazzoni, who had agreed to rejoin Ferrari for 1974, recommended that the Scuderia should sign Lauda as well. And that's just what they did.

General Knowledge IV

G31

How many children of F1 world champions have won the world championship?

B.   Two

Only two drivers have replicated their father's feat in winning the world championship: Damon Hill in 1996 and Nico Rosberg in 2016.

Damon's father, Graham Hill won the championship in 1962 and 1968, and Nico's father, Keke Rosberg, claimed it in 1982.

We may have to wait a while, however, before a third-generation world champion emerges: Damon Hill's son, Josh, did race for a time but left the sport to pursue a career in music. And although Nico Rosberg has two children, the older of them is only five years of age.

G32

For which of the following teams did 1978 world champion Mario Andretti NOT drive.

C.   Brabham

Mario Andretti drove for six different teams in a Formula One career that spanned 14 years and 128 race starts.

Fittingly, given that he was born in Italy, he ended his Formula One career at the wheel of a Ferrari, taking pole position at Monza in his penultimate Grand Prix at the age of 42. His greatest successes in F1 came, however, with Lotus, for whom he took eleven of his twelve Grand Prix wins. He also drove in F1 for Alfa Romeo, March, Parnelli and (as a one-race stand-in) Williams.

There was, however, much more to Andretti's career than Formula One: he won four IndyCar championships and scored race wins in both NASCAR and the World Sportscar Championship. Moroever, he is the only man to have won the F1 world championship and both the Indianapolis and Daytona 500s. And in 1995 he came agonisingly close to adding the Le Mans 24 hours to his list of victories.

G33

Apart from Nino Farina, who is the only driver to have won a Grand Prix at the first attempt?

D.   Giancarlo Baghetti

Having qualified twelfth for the 1961 French Grand Prix in his privately entered Ferrari, Baghetti made steady progress up the order.

Following the retirement of the works Ferraris, he found himself in a late-race scrap with Porsche's Dan Gurney for the lead. They passed and re-passed each other several times, with Gurney a fraction ahead of Baghetti as they started the final lap. They swapped places one last time during that lap, Baghetti taking the chequered flag just 0.1seconds to the good.

Baghetti raced in a further 20 Grands Prix over the next six years, but never again finished in a podium position.

G34

Who is the only driver to have won the F1 world championship, the Le Mans 24 Hours and the Indianapolis 500?

B.   Graham Hill

For 48 years (at the time of writing), Graham Hill has stood alone as the only man to have won the F1 World Drivers' Championship (a feat he accomplished in both 1962 and 1968), the Indianapolis 500 (1966) and the Le Mans 24 Hours (1972). His nearest rival in that sense is Mario Andretti who, having triumphed in F1 in 1978 and won the Indy 500 in 1969, came close to completing the set in 1995, when he finished second at Le Mans.

In more recent times, Fernando Alonso has won both the F1 World Drivers' Championship (2005 and 2006) and the Le Mans 24 Hours. He is keen to add the Indianapolis 500 to his list of victories, and to that end has driven in it in both 2017 and 2020.

G35

Who was the first Swiss driver to win a Grand Prix?

C.   Jo Siffert

Jo Siffert achieved a rare double when he took the chequered flag at the British Grand Prix in 1968, for not only did he become the first Swiss driver to win a world championship Grand Prix (he had previously won three non-championship races) but his victory, at the wheel of Rob Walker's Lotus 49, is also widely regarded as the last by a privately entered car. He went on to win the 1971 Austrian Grand Prix for BRM before being killed in a non-championship race at Brands Hatch.

Siffert's achievements as an F1 driver were at least matched by his success in the World Sportscar Championship, in which he won a number of races including the Daytona 24 Hours, the Sebring 12 Hours and the Targa Florio.

Following his death, the 'Prix Rouge et Blanc Jo Siffert' was instituted. Backed by a tobacco company, the prize took the form of a small gold ingot which was awarded after each Grand Prix to the driver who had, in the opinion of a panel of motorsport journalists, shown the most fighting spirit in that race.

G36

For which of the following teams did Jos Verstappen NOT race in F1?

A.   Jordan

Jos Verstappen joined the Formula One circus in 1994 following highly impressive seasons in Formula Opel Lotus and Formula 3, winning the European championship in the former and the German championship in the latter.

He was initially contracted as Benetton test driver for the 1994 season but stepped up to the race seat in place of J.J. Lehto. His debut season is best remembered for a spectacular fuel fire during a pit stop at the German Grand Prix. But unlike his car, his F1 career never caught fire, and he moved from team to team (he raced for Simtek, Stewart, Tyrrell, Footwork, Arrows and Minardi and tested for Jordan and Honda) over the next few seasons, showing occasional flashes of speed in relatively uncompetitive equipment.

He last drove in F1 in 2003, after which he raced in the A1 Grand Prix series and, later, the Le Mans Series, in which he won his class at the Le Mans 24 Hours.

G37

'Mineral Water' is the English translation of the name of a corner on which circuit?

B.   Imola

Named after the park in which the circuit is situated, *Acque Minerali* (it sounds much nicer in Italian) is a series of two right hand and one left hand corners on the Imola Grand Prix circuit.

The first part of the complex is a downhill right-hand turn which leads into a short straight followed by an uphill right/left combination. The track then continues to climb sharply until it reaches its highest point, '*Variante Alta*' ('high chicane' in English).

Like the *Eau Rouge/Raidillon* complex at Spa, the elevation change at *Acque Minerali* is much more pronounced than it appears on television. Likewise, it's a great place to watch an F1 car go through its paces.

G38

With whom does Lewis Hamilton share the record for the most Grand Prix wins in a debut season?

B.   Jacques Villeneuve

Both Jacques Villeneuve and Lewis Hamilton had the good fortune to start their F1 careers with teams that could supply them with competitive machinery.

Their early F1 careers are similar, in that they both scored four Grand Prix wins en route to finishing runner-up in the world championship in their respective debut seasons. Moreover, they both went on to win the world championship in their second seasons in F1.

There is one final coincidence, in that both men moved teams when many thought the wiser course of action would have been to stay where they were. But that's where the similarities end, with the two men's careers thereafter having followed very different arcs.

G39

Why was Patrick Depailler's 1979 season cut short?

A.   He had a hang-gliding accident

Patrick Depailler was lying joint-third in the championship, having won the Spanish Grand Prix, when he badly broke both legs in a hang-gliding accident during the F1 summer break in 1979.

A lover of challenging sports, Depailler had previously broken a leg in a motorcycle accident shortly after being offered an F1 drive with Tyrrell for the North American races in 1973. In spite of this, Tyrrell signed him up for 1974 but inserted a clause in his contract that prohibited him from certain types of activity. When Depailler moved to Ligier for the 1979 season, however, no such clause was inserted in his contract.

Although not fully recovered from his injuries, Depailler joined the Alfa Romeo team for 1980 and was as committed as ever behind the wheel.

Tragically, he was killed during a private test session at Hockenheim that year when a suspension component broke on the approach to the high-speed *Ostkurve*. With bitter irony, the catch-fencing that might have saved his life sat behind the crash barriers, awaiting installation for the Grand Prix scheduled for the following weekend.

G40

How many Brazilian drivers have won a Grand Prix?

D.   Six

Although a handful of Brazilian drivers drove in F1 in the 1950s, it wasn't until Emerson Fittipaldi made his debut for Team Lotus in 1970 that the nation made a significant impact in Formula One.

With Team Lotus reeling after the death of Jochen Rindt at Monza, Fittipaldi became the team's number one driver for the rest of the season. He shouldered his new role well, winning (albeit by virtue of some good fortune) at Watkins Glen in only his fifth Grand Prix start.

His 1971 season was disappointing, but he bounced back by taking five victories – and the world championship – in 1972, followed by another three victories in 1973. He won the championship again in 1974, this time in a McLaren, and was runner-up in 1975.

He would almost certainly have added to his tally of wins had he not decided to leave the McLaren team at the height of his powers. For the rest of his F1 career, he raced for the Fittipaldi team he had formed with his older brother, Wilson. He never won another Grand Prix and only ascended the podium twice in his final five seasons in F1.

Fittipaldi was followed into the Grand Prix winners' circle by Carlos Pace, who took victory in his home Grand Prix for Brabham in 1975. A talented driver, it's likely that Pace would have added to that single victory had he not been killed in a light aircraft crash shortly after the start of the 1977 F1 season.

Given that Pace was under contract to Brabham at the time of his death, it's therefore appropriate that the next Brazilian to win in F1, Nelson Piquet, would enjoy a great deal of success with that team.

Having joined Brabham for the 1979 season, Piquet took three Grand Prix wins in 1980, finishing second in the championship. He went one better in 1981, and thereafter took his second championship for the team in 1983. He moved to Williams for 1986 and won his third and final championship the following year.

Piquet was still with Brabham when an even more talented Brazilian joined the ranks of Grand Prix winners: Ayrton Senna.

Senna won six Grands Prix for Lotus from 1985 to 1987 before joining McLaren, with whom he would win a further 38 Grands Prix and three world championships. He would undoubtedly have added to both scores but for his fatal crash at Imola in 1994.

Imola nearly claimed the life of another Brazilian, Rubens Barrichello, that weekend, his Jordan becoming airborne over the kerbs at the *Variante Bassa* and hitting the top of the tyre barriers at around 140 miles per hour before landing on its nose and rolling over, ending up on its side. Barrichello was knocked out but miraculously escaped serious injury. Unfortunately, neither Roland Ratzenberger nor Senna were so fortunate in the two days that followed Barrichello's accident.

Barrichello went on to race for Ferrari, where he partnered Michael Schumacher for six seasons. He took nine Grand Prix wins during that time and added two more for Brawn in 2009. He retired from F1 at the end of the 2011 season, eighteen years after making his F1 debut. He started 322 Grands Prix in his career, which remains a record as at the time of writing.

Barrichello was replaced at Ferrari by another Brazilian, Felipe Massa. Having won Grands Prix in both 2006 and 2007, Massa came agonisingly close to winning the world championship in 2008, losing out to Lewis Hamilton by a single point.

Massa then, like Barrichello, survived a serious accident. During qualifying for the 2009 Hungarian Grand Prix, a suspension component fell off Barichello's car, bounced down the track and struck Massa's crash helmet. The impact knocked him out, causing his Ferrari to plough into tyre barriers. He sustained serious head injuries and missed the rest of the

2009 season.

Although he returned in 2010, it's probably fair to say that Massa was (understandably) never quite the same driver after his accident. Even so, he scored eleven Grand Prix victories in his career and earned a great deal of respect, both for the way in which he conducted himself after losing the championship on the final lap of his home Grand Prix in 2008 and for the fortitude he showed in returning to racing after sustaining life-threatening injuries.

General Knowledge V

G41

For which team did Sebastian Vettel make his Grand Prix debut?

B.   BMW Sauber

As BMW Sauber's third driver, Vettel replaced the injured Robert Kubica at the 2007 US Grand Prix, qualifying in seventh position and finishing eighth in the race.

Kubica was back for the next race, but Vettel was soon drafted into the Toro Rosso team to replace Scott Speed. He stayed with the team for 2008, taking pole position for the Italian Grand Prix and going on to win the race, thereby taking Toro Rosso's only Grand Prix victory.

Vettel was promoted to the Red Bull team in 2009, winning four Grands Prix and finishing second in the world championship in his first season.

G42

Which F1 car has won the most Grands Prix in a single season?

C.   Mercedes W07

All four cars have stellar records, with the MP4-4 notching fifteen wins in sixteen Grands Prix, the F2002 winning fifteen out of seventeen, and the F2004 taking fifteen victories in eighteen races. But it's the Mercedes W07 that takes the cake, with drivers Nico Rosberg and Lewis Hamilton winning nineteen of the twenty Grands Prix in 2016.

The chances are that the W07 would have won all twenty races had Hamilton and Rosberg not collided with each other on the first lap of the Spanish Grand Prix. But whilst the chance of setting one record – that of a single car winning every round of the championship – was lost, another record was set that day, with Max Verstappen becoming, at eighteen years old, the youngest ever winner of a Grand Prix.

In terms of sustained success, however, no modern F1 car is likely to ever approach the Lotus 72's record of winning two Drivers' Championships – Rindt in 1970 and Fittipaldi in 1972 - and three Constructors' Championships: 1970, 1972 and 1973.

They don't make 'em like they used to!

G43

Who is the only driver to have scored multiple Grands Prix wins but no other podium finishes?

C.   Jean-Pierre Jabouille

The 1976 European Formula 2 champion, in a car which he designed, Jean-Pierre Jabouille achieved a few firsts in his career.

He was not only the first man to race a turbocharged car in a Grand Prix but also became the first man to win a Grand Prix in one. In so doing, he also became the first French driver to win a Grand Prix in a French car powered by a French engine fed by French fuel and running on French tyres.

Jabouille went on to take a second Grand Prix win in his turbocharged Renault and might well have taken a couple more had his car been more reliable. At the very least, he would have scored a few podium finishes to add his to two wins.

As it was, those two wins were the only times that he finished a Grand Prix in a podium position, thus making him the first (and so far only) multiple Grand Prix winner to have never finished in either of the two lesser podium positions.

G44

Who replaced Niki Lauda at Brabham during the 1979 season?

D.   Ricardo Zunino

Given that Lauda had travelled to Canada and drove the new Ford-powered Brabham BT 49B for a few laps in practice for the Grand Prix, his decision to retire with immediate effect took everyone by surprise.

For Bernie Ecclestone, the owner of the Brabham team, it meant having to find a driver who could take Lauda's place right away.

That man turned out to be Ricardo Zunino, an Argentinian driver who had been competing in the British Formula One championship. Zunino, who was in Canada to watch the race, had recently tested for Brabham and was thus the ideal man to replace Lauda at short notice.

Zunino qualified nineteenth in Canada and finished seventh, several laps down, in a race of attrition. He went better at Watkins Glen, qualifying ninth. And although he spun off during the race, he had done enough to be retained by the team for 1980.

Unfortunately for Zunino, he never came close to matching team-mate Nelson Piquet's pace in 1980, invariably qualifying ten or more places behind him. He lost his place in the Brabham team to Hector Rebaque after the French Grand Prix and was unable to find another drive that season.

He returned to Brabham to contest the non-championship South African Grand Prix in 1981 - it was originally due to have been the opening round of the world championship but became a casualty of the ongoing war between the sport's governing body, FISA, and FOCA, who represented most of the F1 teams.

Having done so, he then drove for Tyrrell in the Brazilian and Argentinian Grands Prix that season. Those two races were, however, his last in F1.

G45

What is the smallest ever margin of victory in the World Drivers' Championship?

B.   0.5 points

A single point has determined the destination of the championship on no fewer than eight occasions, including two consecutive years: 2007 and 2008.

In 1984, however, Niki Lauda won the championship by half a point from McLaren team-mate Alain Prost. Both McLaren drivers were quick off the mark, Prost winning the first Grand Prix of the season, and Lauda taking the second.

That win was, however, Lauda's only points score in the first four races of the championship, and with Prost having won two races and finished second in another, he was fifteen points ahead of the Austrian by the French Grand Prix. Lauda won that one and thereafter the season became a game of swings and roundabouts, with Lauda's guile and experience matched up against the speed of Prost.

Prost's lead in the championship lasted until the Austrian Grand Prix, the twelfth round in the championship.

In that race, the two McLarens engaged in Piquet in a three-way scrap for the lead until lap 29, when oil on the track caused Prost to spin off the circuit and out of the race. Lauda kept up the pressure on Piquet, passing him with 12 laps to go to win his home race for the first time and take the lead of the championship. Prost fought back, winning three of the last four races, but Lauda did just enough to take his third and final world championship by half a point.

And if you're wondering where the half point came from, the answer is Monaco. The heavens opened on race day in the Principality, resulting in a race in which two up and coming young drivers came to the fore: Ayrton Senna and Stefan Bellof, both of whom had grounds for arguing that the victory would have been theirs but for the race director's decision to halt the race after only thirty-one of the scheduled seventy-seven laps had been completed. The result was that half points were awarded, meaning that Prost, who won the race, received 4.5 rather than 9 points (a win was worth 9 points back then) for his efforts.

The duo returned to the fray the following season, but whilst Lauda had a torrid year, winning only one race and amassing a mere fourteen points,

Prost took five victories and his first world championship.

G46

As at the end of the 2019 season, how many drivers have won the world championship?

A.   33

As at the end of 2019, the Drivers' World Championship has been contested seventy times. Of those seventy titles, forty-one have been won by just ten drivers, with Michael Schumacher heading the list with seven championships to his name.

Alberto Ascari was the first multiple world champion, winning the title in both 1952 and 1953. It's likely that he would have added to that number had he not perished when testing a sportscar in 1955. As it is, he remains the last Italian driver to have won the title, although 1978 world champion Mario Andretti was born in what was then part of Italy (and is now part of Croatia).

Drivers from fourteen different countries have won the world championship, with ten British drivers having won the championship a total of nineteen times - a particularly impressive feat when one considers that no other country can lay claim to having produced more than three world champions.

G47

How many times has the world championship been won by a driver who scored only one race victory that season?

B.   Twice

Mike Hawthorn (1958) and Keke Rosberg (1982).

Consistency was the key to Mike Hawthorn's title win in 1958, as he finished second on no fewer than five occasions in addition to his race win. The drivers who finished immediately behind him in the championship standings, Stirling Moss and Tony Brooks, respectively won four and three Grands Prix that season but lost out through finishing fewer races.

The scoring system then in use has been criticised for undervaluing race wins, for which a driver received eight points, only two more than for finishing second. It's worth noting, however, that Hawthorn would still have won the championship if the current scoring system had then been in use.

Finland's Keke Rosberg is the only other driver to have won the championship with just a single race victory to his name that season. Rosberg's victory came in 1982, a season marred by tragedy and controversy, and in which no driver won more than two Grands Prix.

G48

Former Brabham designer Gordon Murray also designed which supercar?

B.   McLaren F1

After leaving Brabham in 1986, Murray joined McLaren as Technical Director. Working alongside Steve Nichols and the rest of the design team, Murray played a part in designing a string of cars that netted multiple world championships for the Woking-based team.

Murray's role in the McLaren F1 team was not as intensive as it had been at Brabham, as he also worked on a road car for the company. This car, with its three-abreast seating and BMW V12 engine made extensive use of high-tech materials such as carbonfibre, titanium and Kevlar.

Styled by Peter Stevens, the car, appropriately called the McLaren F1, was launched in 1992 to a rapturous reception from both the automotive media and the very lucky few able to meet its asking price of over £500,000.

Although primarily a road car, McLaren developed a racing version of the F1, the GTR. Ultimately, twenty-eight GTRs were built, one of which won the 1995 Le Mans 24 Hours.

In total, 106 F1s were built. They remain highly sought after, commanding prices in excess of £10,000,000.

G49

Who is the only driver to have led a Grand Prix in a Minardi?

D.   Pierluigi Martini

Between 1985 and 2005, Minardi (in a variety of guises) competed in 346 Grands Prix, taking the start in 340 of them.

During that time, the team gave Formula One debuts to a number of drivers who went on to greater success, including Fernando Alonso, Mark Webber, Giancarlo Fisichella, Jarno Trulli and Alessandro Nannini.

It was, however, a driver that didn't make the step up that he deserved who holds the distinction of being the only person ever to lead a Grand Prix in a Minardi: Pierluigi Martini.

If ever there was a team stalwart, Martini was it. Of the 118 Grands Prix which Martini started, 102 were at the wheel of a Minardi. Along the way, he became the only man ever to qualify a Minardi on the front row of the grid for a Grand Prix, scored the team's equal best-ever race finish (fourth), and in Portugal in 1989 he actually led the race itself. Admittedly, his lead lasted only a single lap and was aided by the leaders having made their first pit stops.

Always a small team, Minardi became something of a favourite with F1 fans. And although it ceased to exist when Red Bull purchased it in 2005, its successor (Toro Rosso, now Alpha Tauri) has retained not only its base at Faenza but something of the team's tradition of bringing through young drivers.

G50

In how many seasons has the same driver won both the first and last Grands Prix?

B.   20

As might be expected, history shows that the driver who won both the first and last Grands Prix of a season usually also won the world championship. Indeed, the record books show that the first three world champions (Farina, Fangio and Ascari) all won the first and last races of their championship seasons.

Stirling Moss was the first driver to win the first and last races in a season (1958) without also winning the championship. He was followed in this regard by Jackie Stewart (1972), Alan Jones (1981), Alain Prost (1984 and 1988) and Jenson Button (2012). Curiously, Stewart, Prost and Button all failed to win both the first and last races in any of their championship seasons.

As for Moss, he remains the only driver to have won the races that bookended a season without ever becoming world champion.

General Knowledge VI

G51

What is Nico Hulkenberg's best race finish in F1?

A.   Fourth

Nico Hulkenberg currently holds the record for the most Grands Prix started without finishing in a podium position.

In his 177 Grand Prix starts to date*, his best finish in a Grand Prix is fourth. He has done so on three occasions, most recently in the 2016 Belgian Grand Prix.

Given his extremely impressive record in junior formulae, in which he won races and championships in Formula BMW, A1 Grand Prix, Formula 3 and GP2, it can be argued that Hulkenberg's disappointing record in F1 says more about the quality of the equipment at his disposal than his ability as a driver.

*As at the end of 2019. He has since added one to that tally as a stand-in driver.

G52

For which team did Paul di Resta make a one-off appearance in 2017?

D.   Williams

Having spent three seasons with the Force India team, Paul di Resta found himself without an F1 drive for the 2014 season.

He thereafter spent two seasons away from F1 before being appointed reserve driver for Williams in 2016. He did not drive in any of the Grands Prix that year but made a one-off return at the 2017 Hungarian Grand Prix, when he replaced an unwell Felipe Massa. The timing of the switch meant that Di Resta was thrown straight into qualifying without having participated in any of the practice sessions.

In spite of his unfamiliarity with the car, Di Resta was able to qualify in 19th position, a little over three-quarters of a second slower than his team-mate, Lance Stroll. He retired from the race after 60 laps due to an oil leak.

Massa returned for the next race, and Di Resta has not since driven in a Grand Prix.

G53

Which of these drivers contested the most Grands Prix for Toro Rosso?

B.   Sébastien Buemi

With 55 Grand Prix starts for Toro Rosso to his name, Sébastien Buemi drove in as many Grands Prix for the team as Scott Speed and Sebastian Bourdais combined, and in nine more than his erstwhile team-mate, Jaime Alguersuari.

In the three seasons he drove for Toro Rosso, from 2009 to 2011, Buemi's best finish in a Grand Prix was seventh, a feat he managed on two occasions, both in 2009.

After leaving Toro Rosso, he raced in both Formula E and the World Endurance Championship, meeting with considerable success. He won the Formula E championship in 2015-16 and has twice been runner-up in the series.

He went one better in the World Endurance Championship, winning it in both 2016 and 2018-19 as well as twice winning the Le Mans 24 Hours.

Of the other Toro Rosso alumni, both Scott Speed and Sebastien Bourdais have enjoyed some measure of success – Speed having won several rallycross championships, and Bourdais having added to his tally of race wins in IndyCar.

Jaime Alguersuari followed a different path, however, and retired from motorsport at the age of 25, his potential unfulfilled.

G54

Who set the first sub-7 minute lap of the Nürburgring Nordschleife in an F1 car?

A.   Niki Lauda

Lauda was well on his way to winning his first world championship in 1975 when he took pole position for the German Grand Prix. He was the only driver to better 7 minutes in qualifying, setting a time of 6 minutes 58.6 seconds for a lap of the 14.189 mile Nürburgring Nordschleife.

He'd have won the race too, but for a puncture that dropped him down the order. Even so, the points he got for finishing third ensured that he left the Nürburgring with a substantial lead in the championship standings.

It's likely that Lauda's qualifying mark would have been bettered in 1976, but bad weather meant that the grid positions were decided on the basis of the times set in the Friday qualifying session, none of which came close to Lauda's 1975 pole time.

The German Grand Prix moved to Hockenheim in 1977. Although F1 has since returned to the Nürburgring on several occasions, it has used the 3.2 mile long GP-Strecke circuit built in the 1980s rather than the much more daunting Nordschleife.

G55

Which of the following drivers won their first Grand Prix in the fewest attempts?

B.   Jacques Villeneuve

Villeneuve led much of his first F1 race, the 1996 Australian Grand Prix, but a damaged oil line, possibly resulting from an off-track excursion, caused him to have to slow with five laps left to run and allow team-mate Damon Hill past to take the win. Villeneuve was, however, able to keep his engine running long enough to make the finish line and take second place on his debut.

He recorded his first Grand Prix victory three races later and followed it up by notching a further three victories that season.

Eleven years later, Lewis Hamilton became the first driver since Villeneuve to finish in a podium position on his Grand Prix debut. Hamilton's third place in Australia was followed up by four consecutive second places before he won the the Canadian Grand Prix, the first of his seven victories (so far) in that event. Like Villeneuve, he would win three more Grands Prix in his debut season and finish second in the world championship.

Sebastian Vettel made his Grand Prix debut in the same season as Hamilton, driving for BMW Sauber at the United States Grand Prix before switching to Toro Rosso for the final seven Grands Prix of the year.

He stayed with the Faenza-based outfit for 2008, making the best of the weather conditions at Monza by taking both pole position and victory in the Italian Grand Prix. It was his twenty-second Grand Prix and Toro Rosso's first Grand Prix finish in a podium position. It would remain the team's only podium finish until the 2019 season.

Fernando Alonso's first season in F1 was at the wheel of a Minardi in 2001. He impressed, but there was no prospect of scoring points in a Minardi let alone winning a Grand Prix.

Alonso thereafter spent a year as a test driver for the Renault team before making the step up to their race team in 2003. And although the Renault was seldom a match for the Ferrari, Williams and McLaren cars, Alonso took it to victory at the Hungarian Grand Prix in his twenty-ninth Grand Prix start.

G56

Who took the only pole position for the Toleman team?

B.   Teo Fabi

1984 had been a great year for Toleman, with a Brazilian rookie named Ayrton Senna taking three podiums and the team finishing in seventh place (out of seventeen teams) in the constructors' championship.

The following season did not, however, bring much in the way of results or joy for the Witney-based team. Senna had gone, joining Lotus in spite of a contract that bound him to Toleman for both 1985 and 1986. Moreover, the team found itself without a tyre supplier and had to sit out the first three races of the season.

On the plus side, Italian clothing company Benetton came in as the team's main sponsor and resolved the tyre situation by purchasing Spirit Racing's tyre contract with Pirelli and assigning it to Toleman.

The team's replacement for Senna, Teo Fabi, turned in a handful of good performances in qualifying, scoring the team's first and only pole position at the German Grand Prix. That was, however, as good as it got, and poor reliability meant that neither he nor team-mate Piercarlo Ghinzani scored any world championship points.

The team was purchased by Benetton at the end of the 1985 season and went on to win two world championships with Michael Schumacher in 1994 and 1995 before being purchased by Renault.

G57

Which of the following Grands Prix did Michael Schumacher never win?

D.   Turkey

Michael Schumacher's ninety-one Grand Prix victories were achieved on twenty-three circuits in eighteen countries.

Although he took multiple wins in a number of Grands Prix (most notably Canada, where he was victorious eight times), he won only once in Argentina (in four attempts), once in Portugal (in five attempts), once in Bahrain (again, in five attempts) and once in China (in six attempts).

Apart from the South African Grand Prix, which he contested twice early in his F1 career, the only Grand Prix that he failed to win between his debut in 1991 and his first retirement at the end of 2006 was the Turkish Grand Prix.

He contested the race twice: in 2005, when his Ferrari was uncompetitive, and in 2006, when he finished third after having to double-stack behind team-mate Felipe Massa at a pit stop triggered by the deployment of the Safety Car.

G58

For which team did Jonathan Palmer make his F1 debut?

C.   Williams

If you were to look only at his statistics an F1 driver, you might form the impression that Jonathan Palmer was an also-ran. If so, you'd be wrong, for Palmer is very much one of life's achievers.

His early adult life saw him split his time between his medical studies and motor sport. And he was successful in both, qualifying and working as a medical doctor and progressing through the ranks to Formula 1, winning both the British F3 championship and European F2 championship along the way.

In 1982, he combined Formula 2 with his first role in F1, that of a test driver for Williams. His commitments remained the same for 1983, but in this season he not only won the European F2 championship but was also given his F1 debut by Williams in the European Grand Prix at Brands Hatch.

Palmer raced in F1 for the RAM team in 1984 and thereafter drove for Zakspeed in seven Grands Prix in 1985 before undertaking a full season with the team in 1986.

There was some talk that Palmer might join McLaren as Prost's number two for 1987, but instead he ended up at Tyrrell. It would prove to be his best year in F1, for although the Tyrrell was somewhat underpowered it was both nimble and reliable, and Palmer took three points finishes in it.

He remained with the team for 1988, once again finishing in the points in three occasions. His final season in F1 was in 1989, when he took his Tyrrell to two sixth places.

He enjoyed greater success in sportscar racing, finishing second in the 1985 Le Mans 24 Hours and winning the 1984 Brands Hatch 1000km, both in a Porsche. He subsequently drove in the BTCC in 1991, finishing seventh in the championship.

That same year, he took his first steps into the business side of motorsport, founding PalmerSport. He followed this up by joining forces with two partners to set up MotorSport Vision.

Since its foundation in 2004, MSV has become a key player in British motorsport. It owns and operates several major British circuits, including Brands Hatch and Donington, as well as operating a number of racing series on two and four wheels, including the BRDC British F3 championship and the British Superbike Championship.

His son, Jolyon Palmer, also made it to F1 and raced in 35 Grands Prix for Renault in 2016 and 2017.

G59

Who among these drivers took the most pole positions in F1?

D.   Alain Prost

Although better known for his race pace, Alain Prost nonetheless took 33 pole positions during his F1 career: 13 for Williams (1993), ten for McLaren (1984 to 1989), and ten for Renault (1981 to 1983). Curiously, although Prost won five Grands Prix for Ferrari in 1990, he failed to score a single pole position for the team in either that year or in 1991.

Of the other drivers listed, Nigel Mansell took thirty-two pole positions, Nelson Piquet twenty-three, and Fernando Alonso, another driver better known for his performance in races, twenty-two.

As it stands at the end of the 2019 season, Prost is tied for fifth place with

Jim Clark in terms of the number of pole positions taken. That list is headed by Lewis Hamilton, with 88 poles, followed by Michael Schumacher (68), Ayrton Senna (65) and Sebastian Vettel (57).

G60

Which French circuit featured a cobbled hairpin?

A.   Rouen-les-Essarts

The French Grand Prix was first run at Rouen in 1952, and the circuit would go on to host it on a further four occasions.

Formed out of public roads, the circuit was just over four miles long (after 1955) and had a distinctive character, its layout featuring a series of sweeping downhill S-bends that called on both courage and precision, the cobbled *Nouveau Monde* hairpin, and a long uphill stretch with a gradient that reached 1:11 in places.

It last hosted a Grand Prix in 1968, when Jo Schlesser was killed after his magnesium-skinned Honda RA302 crashed at the tricky *Six Frères* section of the circuit.

Five years later, the same section of the circuit claimed the life of talented Scottish driver Gerry Birrell, whose F2 car suffered a puncture and slid into a crash barrier that hadn't been properly secured.

Had Birrell lived, he might well have replaced Jackie Stewart at Tyrrell for 1974. Those who knew him speak of a potential world champion cut down before his time.

In any event, Birrell seemed destined for great things outside of motor racing. As an engineer and test driver, his work included undertaking much of the suspension development for Ford on the original Escort RS2000, which was launched shortly after his death.

As for Rouen, it ceased to operate in the early 1990s. The old pits and grandstands lingered a while longer, as did the cobbles at *Nouveau Monde*. All are, however, long gone now.

General Knowledge VII

G61

Who was the first driver to start 200 Grands Prix?

A.   Riccardo Patrese

Patrese's F1 career began at the Monaco Grand Prix in 1977 and ended at the Australian Grand Prix in 1993. Along the way he drove for Shadow, Arrows, Brabham (two spells), Alfa Romeo, Williams and Benetton.

In all, Patrese started 256 Grands Prix, winning six of them and finishing in one of the lesser podium positions a further thirty-one times.

In his early days, Patrese had a reputation for overly aggressive driving. In 1978, he was unjustly blamed for causing the start-line collision at Monza that ultimately claimed the life of Ronnie Peterson. Indeed, several of his fellow drivers demanded that he be suspended from driving in the next Grand Prix. The furore was such that Patrese's team decided to withdraw his entry from that race.

Three years later, Patrese and the race director of the 1978 Italian Grand Prix stood trial in Italy on manslaughter charges relating to Peterson's death. They were both acquitted.

Patrese overcame these early tribulations and went on to become a popular and much-respected member of the F1 community.

G62

At which of these circuits was the 1950 Grand Prix won at the highest average speed?

C.   Spa-Francorchamps

The old 8 mile Spa circuit was exciting, dangerous and very fast. In 1950, Fangio won the Belgian Grand Prix at an average of 110.043 miles per hour, narrowly beating Farina's winning average of 109.699 mph at Monza.

Reims-Gueux was also a fast circuit, with the 1950 GP being won at an average of over 104 mph. Silverstone, however, lagged some distance behind, with Farina winning at an average of 'only' 90.963 mph.

For outright speed, however, the fastest circuit on the calendar was, of course, the banked oval of the Indianapolis Motor Speedway, with that year's '500' (which, although run under different rules to the other races, counted towards the F1 world championship) being won at an average speed of 124.002 mph.

G63

Who scored the last Grand Prix victory for a 12-cylinder engine?

C.   Jean Alesi

Although 12-cylinder engines had once been fairly commonplace in F1, they had fallen out of favour by the mid-1990s. Indeed, by 1994, only Ferrari was still using a 12-cylinder engine, although they had plans to replace it with a V10 engine midway through the 1995 season.

As it happened, the V10 engine didn't appear until the first Grand Prix of 1996, leaving Jean Alesi and Gerhard Berger to soldier on with the sonorous but thirsty V12 throughout 1995. The high point of that season came in Canada, when Alesi passed Michael Schumacher's ailing Benetton to take the sole victory of his career, and that on his 31st birthday.

G64

In what year was the South African Grand Prix last run?

B.   1993

The South African Grand Prix was first run as a round of the world championship in 1962, when Jim Clark's Lotus retired with victory in

234

sight, thereby handing both the race and world championship to BRM's Graham Hill.

That race and the next two, in 1963 and 1965, were held at the Prince George circuit in East London. After a final, non-championship F1 race at East London in 1966, the South African Grand Prix moved to a new home in 1967: the Kyalami circuit near Johannesburg.

That first Grand Prix at Kyalami nearly threw up a shock winner: John Love in a privately entered Cooper. Love, who had qualified in fifth position, inherited the lead on lap 59 out of 80 and held it until seven laps from the end, when he had to stop to take on more fuel. He eventually finished second to works Cooper driver Pedro Rodriguez, who scored his first Grand Prix win.

Jim Clark took his final Grand Prix win at Kyalami in 1968, and over the years the circuit was the scene of some great races: Ronnie Peterson's last-lap win in 1978, the race-long battle between the Ferraris in 1979, and Alain Prost's remarkable comeback victory in 1982.

It was also, alas, the scene of Peter Revson's fatal testing crash in 1974 and the tragic death of Tom Pryce and a young marshal, Jansen van Vuuren, in 1977.

Throughout most its existence, the South African Grand Prix was tainted due to the country's racial segregation, a system known as apartheid. Revulsion at this system led to South Africa being banned from competing in most forms of international sport, a process that began in the 1960s. F1, however, continued to visit South Africa until 1985. In that year, two teams – Renault and Ligier – boycotted the race, pressure was brought on other drivers not to compete and some sponsors removed their logos from the cars they usually adorned.

Several days after the race, the FIA announced that F1 would not return to South Africa while apartheid remained.

By 1992, the political landscape in South Africa had radically changed, and the South African Grand Prix returned to the racing calendar. It was held on a much-changed Kyalami circuit, but issues over funding and payment caused it to disappear from the world championship once again after 1993.

G65

Who scored Honda's first Grand Prix victory?

D.   Richie Ginther

Honda made their F1 debut in 1964, running a single car (powered by their own V12 engine) for American Ronnie Bucknum.

For 1965, they embarked on a more extensive racing programme, taking part in eight of the season's ten Grands Prix. Bucknum was retained and was joined by his fellow American, Richie Ginther, who had previously raced for both Ferrari and BRM in F1.

The Honda showed up well in qualifying for much of the season, but results were harder to come by, with the team having amassed just two points before the season-ending Mexican Grand Prix, the final race before a rule change doubled the maximum capacity of F1 engines from 1.5 litres to 3.0 litres.

From third on the grid, Ginther inherited the lead after Jim Clark, Graham Hill and Jackie Stewart retired from the race. Once in the lead, he remained there, fending off Dan Gurney to take his and Honda's first Grand Prix victory and make it a one-two for American drivers.

Ginther continued to race for Honda until the end of the 1966 season. He retired from motor racing in 1967 and died in 1989.

G66

In what year did British drivers finish first, second, third, fourth and fifth-equal in the world championship?

A.   1958

1958 was a remarkable year for British motorsport. With Fangio only competing in only two Grands Prix that season, the door was open for the likes of Moss, Hawthorn, Brooks and Collins to battle for the honour of becoming Britain's first F1 world champion.

It was an invitation that was gladly accepted, with Hawthorn just edging out Moss to win the championship, with Brooks third, Roy Salvadori fourth and Collins a posthumous joint fifth in the standings.

Such was the domination of British drivers that year that they won all but one of the nine Grands Prix (the Indianapolis 500 was not regarded as a Grand Prix) and would almost certainly have won the other, at Monaco, had not technical problems accounted for Hawthorn, Moss and Brooks.

G67

Who did Nick Heidfeld replace at BMW Sauber during the 2010 season?

B.   Pedro de la Rosa

Having driven for BMW Sauber for four seasons, BMW's decision to withdraw from F1 at the end of the 2009 season ultimately left Heidfeld without a race seat for 2010, the newly reconstituted Sauber team (still known as BMW Sauber) having signed Pedro de la Rosa to partner Kamui Kobayashi.

Heidfeld duly joined Mercedes as test driver, but never actually drove the team's W01 car. In August 2010, Mercedes released him from his contract so that he could join Pirelli as the test driver for their F1 tyre project.

In the meantime, de la Rosa was struggling to get the grips with the recalcitrant Sauber C29. With five Grands Prix still to run, Sauber released the Spaniard and signed Nick Heidfeld as his replacement.

Although Heidfeld also found the C29 to be something of a handful, he bettered de la Rosa's performance by twice finishing in the points.

Heidfeld then replaced the injured Robert Kubica, his old BMW Sauber team-mate, at the Lotus Renault team for 2011. But in a reverse of the previous season, he found himself out of a drive during the season.

237

That brought an end to Heidfeld's F1 career, resulting in him leaving the sport as the driver who had scored the most podium positions (13) without ever winning a Grand Prix.

G68

Who was the first driver to win a Grand Prix in three different decades?

A.   Jack Brabham

In an F1 career that spanned fifteen years, Jack Brabham won fourteen Grands Prix and three world championships.

His first Grand Prix victory came at Monaco in 1959, and he also won in Britain that year en route to his first world championship. The 1960s saw him take eleven further Grand Prix victories, nine of which were scored in his world championship winning seasons in 1960 and 1966.

Brabham's final F1 victory came in the season-opening South African Grand Prix in 1970. Though well into his forties, Brabham performed well for much of what would be his final season in F1, losing out on two further victories due to final lap dramas: at Monaco, where he made an error at the final corner when under pressure from Jochen Rindt, and at Brands Hatch, where he ran out of fuel with the finish line in sight.

Brabham's record as the only driver to have won Grands Prix in three different decades lasted until Lewis Hamilton won the 2020 Styrian Grand Prix, thus making him the second man to win across three decades.

It's possible that Brabham and Hamilton could soon be joined in the 'three decade' club, as Sebastian Vettel, Kimi Raikkonen and Fernando Alonso have all already won Grands Prix in each of the two previous decades.

G69

In which year did the Australian Grand Prix start the season, four months after bringing the previous season to a close?

B.   1996

238

The 1995 F1 season concluded with the Australian Grand Prix at Adelaide, the eleventh and final time that the city hosted the race.

Four months later, in March 1996, the Australian Grand Prix kicked-off the new Formula One season. This time, however, the race was run not in Adelaide, but at Albert Park in Melbourne. It has remained there ever since.

And lest you be wondering, Damon Hill won both the 1995 and 1996 races.

G70

Who is the oldest person to have raced in a Grand Prix?

D.   Louis Chiron

Louis Chiron's heyday as a racing driver was during the 1920s and early 1930s, when he won a number of major races, including the 1931 French Grand Prix in a Bugatti which he shared with Achille Varzi. In stark contrast to modern Grands Prix, the duration of the race was ten hours, with the winners covering just under 800 miles in that time.

Chiron won his home Grand Prix at Monaco in 1931 and was leading it in 1932 when he crashed out while attempting to lap another car.

Forty years of age when hostilities commenced in 1939, Chiron resumed his racing career after the war. He won the French Grand Prix twice more in the pre-F1 era and thereafter drove in fifteen Grands Prix between 1950 and 1955, taking third place at the 1950 Monaco Grand Prix.

The Principality was also the locus of his last Grand Prix, in 1955, in which he finished sixth. He took part in practice for the 1958 Monaco Grand Prix, by which time he was 58 years old, but did not start the race.

Chiron later became clerk of the course for the Monaco Grand Prix, famously waving the starting flag not from the safety of a gantry but on the track itself.

The Drivers I

D1

Who is the only driver to have led every Grand Prix in which he raced?

D.   Markus Winkelhock

Markus Winkelhock has an enviable racing pedigree, being the son of former F1 driver Manfred Winkelhock and the nephew of former BTCC champion, Joachim Winkelhock.

Having won races in both F3 and Formula Renault 3.5, Winkelhock was called in to the Spyker F1 team for the 2007 European Grand Prix as a replacement for Christijan Albers. Having had very little time to familiarise himself with his new steed, Winkelhock qualified in 22nd and last place.

That changed within two laps of the race starting. Although rain was expected, all twenty-two cars started their formation laps on dry tyres, and all but one of them were thus equipped at the start. The exception was Winkelhock, his team having called him into the pits for wet weather tyres at the end of the formation lap.

It was a gamble, and it worked. Rain started to fall during the first lap, causing the rest of the field to head for the pits. This, coupled with the fact that many of those who stopped fitted intermediates rather than the full wets which the conditions demanded, meant that Winkelhock, who had no previous experience of wet weather driving in an F1 car, found himself in the led by the end of lap two.

He was leading by over half a minute when the Safety Car was deployed. The race was then red flagged. It was subsequently re-started, but Spyker made the wrong call this time, giving Winkelhock full wet tyres rather than the intermediates that were better suited to the improved track conditions. Winkelhock fell down the order after the re-start and retired after 15 laps with hydraulic problems. For six laps, however, he had done something that neither his father nor his uncle had managed: he led a

240

Grand Prix.

That one appearance marked both the beginning and the end of Winkelhock's F1 career. He went on to race mostly in sports and touring cars, winning both the World GT1 Championship and the Intercontinental GT Challenge.

His shot at F1 glory may have been brief, but he remains the only driver to have led every Grand Prix he contested.

D2

By what title is former Lotus driver Johnny Dumfries also known?

B.   The Marquess of Bute

John Crichton-Stuart, who was then the Earl of Dumfries, drove in F1 for just a single season, a year in which he had the thankless task of being Ayrton Senna's team-mate in a set-up in which he was very much the team's number two driver. Crichton-Stuart chose not to use neither his title nor his given surname and instead raced as 'Johnny Dumfries'.

Senna's dominion over the Lotus team at that time was such that, concerned about the ability of the team to service the needs of two drivers of equal status, he successfully vetoed the appointment of Derek Warwick as his team-mate.

Although Dumfries was a talented driver who had won the British F3 series in 1984 and finished runner-up in the European championship that same year, he struggled in an environment in which the team's focus was very much on Senna.

His services were dispensed with for 1987, as Lotus took on Satoru Nakajima to partner Senna, a consequence of the deal that secured a supply of Honda engines for the team.

But although it marked the end of the F1 road for Dumfries, he continued to race until the early 1990s, winning the 1988 Le Mans 24 Hours for Jaguar with team-mates Andy Wallace and Jan Lammers.

One final thing: he still doesn't use his title. Since inheriting his current title, he's been known simply as 'Johnny Bute'.

D3

For which team did Jarno Trulli take his only Grand Prix victory?

A.   Renault

Named after 1970s motorcycle racing star Jarno Saarinen, Trulli was seven years into his F1 career when he took his only Grand Prix victory at Monaco in 2004.

His win, Renault's only victory in 2004, followed a typically brilliant qualifying performance, in which he took pole position by the considerable (in Monaco terms) margin of 0.36 seconds.

His Monaco triumph notwithstanding, Trulli's relationship with Renault Team Principal Flavio Briatore turned sour that season, and he was sacked with three Grands Prix left to run. He thereafter joined Toyota, for whom he scored several podium finishes over the next few years but no further victories.

D4

How many Scottish drivers have won a Grand Prix?

B.   Four

Jim Clark (25 wins), Jackie Stewart (27) and David Coulthard (13) were preceded by Innes Ireland, who won the 1961 United States Grand Prix.

Ireland's victory made him the first man to win a Grand Prix for Team Lotus. It came in what proved to be his last race for the team, who thereafter dispensed with his services in favour of his fellow Scot, Jim Clark. Ireland continued to race in F1 for several more seasons, winning no further Grands Prix but taking victory in three non-championship races to add to the five he won with Team Lotus.

A colourful character, Ireland led a rich and varied life outside of racing: he trained as engineer with Rolls-Royce, served in the Suez Canal Zone with the Parachute Regiment, skippered a fishing boat and became a noted motorsport journalist. He died in 1993.

D5

Tyrrell star Francois Cevert's brother-in-law was also an F1 driver. Who was he?

D.   Jean-Pierre Beltoise

Jean-Pierre Beltoise was married to Jacqueline Cevert, whose brother Francois partnered Jackie Stewart at Tyrrell for over three seasons.

Beltoise and Cevert each won just one Grand Prix, although had fate been different one or other of them could conceivably have become France's first world champion: Beltoise was hampered for most of his career by the legacy of a serious injury to his left arm whilst Cevert was killed in practice for the 1973 U.S. Grand Prix. Had he lived, he would have taken over from the retiring Jackie Stewart as the Tyrrell team's lead driver for the 1974 season.

D6

Who did Sebastian Vettel depose as the youngest driver to win the world championship?

C.   Lewis Hamilton

This is one of the few records that Michael Schumacher never held. He would, however, almost certainly have taken the record from Emerson Fittipaldi in 1994 but for his disqualification from the Belgian Grand Prix and his absence from two Grands Prix due to an FIA-imposed suspension. As it was, he did not clinch that year's championship until the last race of the season, by which time he was eleven days older than Fittipaldi had been when he won his first world championship in 1972.

Fittipaldi, who was 25 years and 303 days old when he won the first of his two champions in 1972, held the record for 33 years before it was finally broken by Fernando Alonso, who was 24 years and 59 days old when he took the first of his back-to-back championships in 2005.

Alonso's tenure as record holder lasted only three seasons, with Lewis Hamilton taking it in 2008 at the age of 23 years and 300 days. Hamilton's time as the record holder was even shorter, with Sebastian Vettel taking it in 2010, at the age of 23 years and 134 days.

As an ever-increasing number of talented drivers enter F1 at a young age, it's a record that may well be broken again in the not too distant future.

D7

Which 1970s Grand Prix driver was known as 'the Monza Gorilla'?

C.   Vittorio Brambilla

The fast but not infrequently wild Italian with the bone-crunching handshake raced in 74 Grands Prix between 1974 and 1980, becoming something of a cult hero to F1 fans across the globe.

Although Brambilla came late to F1, being 36 when he made his debut, he showed flashes of genuine speed, particularly in the 1975 season when he led the Belgian Grand Prix for many laps, took pole position in Sweden, and won the rain-shortened Austrian Grand Prix.

He survived a serious head injury sustained in a startline crash at Monza in 1978 and retired from F1 in 1980. He passed away in 2001.

D8

In what year did Nigel Mansell make his Grand Prix debut?

A.   1980

Nigel Mansell's introduction to F1 was quite literally a pain in the backside.

Having impressed Colin Chapman enough to be given a role as test driver for Team Lotus in 1980, Mansell was further rewarded by being granted his Grand Prix debut at that year's Austrian Grand Prix.

His race was, however, as much a test of endurance as of skill, a fuel leak into the cockpit of his Lotus leaving him with painful burns to his posterior. Mansell nonetheless kept going, his race ending only when his engine expired after 40 laps.

He drove for Lotus in two more races that season and thereafter raced for the team until the end of the 1984 season.

D9

How many times did Michael and Ralf Schumacher finish first and second in a Grand Prix?

C.   Five

The brothers notched a total of five 1-2 finishes over the ten seasons in which they raced together in F1.

The first of them came in Canada in 2001, with Ralf leading his older brother home. It was the first time that siblings had finished first and second in a Grand Prix.

The brothers repeated the feat two races later, at the French Grand Prix. This time, however, it was Michael who led the way home. This scenario would be repeated at the 2002 Brazilian Grand Prix, the 2003 Canadian Grand Prix and, finally, the 2004 Japanese Grand Prix.

D10

How many world championship points did Jody Scheckter score in 1980?

A.   Two

Having been competitive in 1979, Ferrari's inability to create a true ground-effect car due to the width of their Flat-12 engine meant that they were very much also-rans in 1980.

Scheckter's team-mate, Gilles Villeneuve, put in some typically head-turning drives that season but even his skill and enthusiasm wasn't enough to turn the tardy Ferrari T5 into a car that could match the Williamses, Ligiers, Renaults and Brabhams.

As for Scheckter, his solitary points finish was a distant fifth place in the United States (West) Grand Prix at Long Beach. Content that he'd achieved his dream of becoming world champion, he retired at the end of that season.

The Drivers II

D11

Who was the first woman to race in a Grand Prix?

B.   Maria Teresa de Filippis

Italian aristocrat Maria Teresa de Filippis started racing at the age of 22, finishing second in the Italian sportscar championship six years later.

In 1958, at the wheel of a Maserati 250F, she qualified for three of the four Grands Prix she entered. She finished in only one of them, taking tenth place in the Belgian Grand Prix. She also raced in the non-championship Syracuse Grand Prix that season, finishing fifth.

Her F1 programme was more limited in 1959, and she failed to qualify for the only Grand Prix (Monaco) which she entered. She did, however, race in the International Trophy at Silverstone but failed to finish.

She retired from motor racing that year. Sixteen years would then pass before a woman again raced in a Grand Prix.

D12

Mike Hawthorn and which other world champion each won three Grands Prix in their career?

D.   Phil Hill

None of the drivers to have won the F1 world championship won fewer than three Grands Prix during their careers. Indeed, of all the world champions only Mike Hawthorn (champion in 1958) and Phil Hill (champion in 1961) ended their careers with fewer than five Grand Prix victories.

To put that into context, it must be remembered that both Hawthorn and Hill started fewer than fifty Grands Prix in their careers. The competition was tough in their eras, too, with Hawthorn having the likes of Fangio, Moss, Collins and Brooks to contend with, and Hill finding himself up against Moss, Clark, Von Trips, Hill, Brabham and Gurney. Even so, Hawthorn racked up eighteen podiums in his career, with Hill finishing a Grand Prix in the top three on sixteen occasions.

The two men, team-mates at Ferrari in 1958, shared the podium twice that season, most significantly in the final Grand Prix of the season.

In that race, Hawthorn found himself needing to finish second to clinch the championship. He spent much of the race in fourth place, which became third after the retirement of Tony Brooks. This became second after Hill, running in second place, allowed Hawthorn to pass him, thus ensuring that the Englishman would become the UK's first F1 world champion.

Hill received no such favours from his team-mate in 1961, being engaged for much of the season in an inter-Ferrari battle for supremacy with Wolfgang von Trips. The battle between the two men ebbed and flowed, with von Trips having edged ahead in the points standings by the time of the penultimate Grand Prix at Monza.

Von Trips took pole for that race, but it was Hill who led from the start. Eager to get back on terms with the American, Von Trips made a small error with catastrophic consequences: the rear left wheel of his Ferrari hit the front right wheel of Jim Clark's Lotus, causing the Ferrari to veer at high speed into a fence on top of an embankment, killing Von Trips and fifteen spectators.

As was generally the case in those days, the race continued in spite of the tragic events. Hill took the win, and with it the world championship, his joy dampened by sadness at the loss of a friend and, though he was utterly blameless, a feeling of guilt.

In a grotesque coincidence, the only other American to win the world championship, Mario Andretti, would also do so at Monza, seventeen years after Hill and in similar circumstances. In Andretti's case, his Lotus team-mate and only remaining rival for the championship, Ronnie Peterson, died as a result of injuries sustained in a start-line crash. As a distraught Andretti told reporters after learning of Peterson's death, "Unfortunately, motor racing is also this."

D13

How many Grands Prix did Niki Lauda win at McLaren?

D.   Eight

Having joined McLaren for the 1982 season, Lauda's first season with the team saw him take two Grand Prix victories en route to fifth place in the championship standings. He found the going somewhat more difficult in 1983, scoring only twelve points and ending the season in tenth place.

Although he had lost out to team-mate John Watson in both 1982 and 1983, Lauda remained with the team for 1984. With Alain Prost having replaced Watson and the McLaren cars now having turbocharged engines, the season promised much in the way of both intrigue and results.

It did not disappoint. The new McLaren MP 4/2 was fast, winning twelve of the sixteen Grands Prix and turning the race for the world championship into a straight battle between Lauda and Prost. The Frenchman held the advantage for much of the season, Lauda's challenge having been somewhat blunted after failing to finish in six of the first nine Grands Prix.

After that disappointing start, Niki then went on a run of seven straight points finishes that saw him win three Grands Prix and finish second on three other occasions. It was enough to give him the championship by half a point from Prost, albeit the Frenchman took seven Grand Prix wins to the five scored by the Austrian.

Unfortunately for Lauda, his defence of the championship in 1985 never got off the ground. He missed two races with a wrist injury, failed to finish in eleven others and scored but a single victory. He retired at the end of the season in spite of his team's desire that he continue to race.

One of the bravest and most intelligent drivers ever to have graced the sport, Niki Lauda passed away in May, 2019, aged 70.

D14

In which year did Denny Hulme win the World Drivers' Championship?

A.   1967

Hulme beat Brabham team-mate (and boss) Jack Brabham by five points to become the first (and so far only) Kiwi to win the world championship. He went on to finish third in the championship standings on two further occasions, winning a total of eight Grands Prix during his career and amassing a further twenty-five podium finishes.

Like most drivers of his era, Hulme was highly versatile. He also won the Can-Am championship twice, finished second (with Ken Miles) in the 1966 Le Mans 24 Hours, losing certain victory due to a Ford PR stunt that backfired, and took a dozen wins in the British Sportscar Championship.

Hulme retired from Formula One at the end of the 1974 season. He returned to New Zealand but continued to race from time to time before making a more serious comeback in the early 1980s. He returned to Europe in 1986 to drive a Rover Vitesse in the European Touring Car Championship, winning the Silverstone round and thereby taking his third win in the Tourist Trophy, eighteen years after his second victory in the event.

In 1992, Hulme suffered a fatal heart attack during the Bathurst 1000 in Australia. He was the first F1 world champion to die of natural causes.

D15

In 1973, the George Medal was awarded to which two British F1 drivers?

B.   Mike Hailwood and David Purley

Awarded for acts of great bravery, the George Medal is primarily intended for civilians rather than military personnel.

Multiple motorcycle world champion and TT winner, Mike Hailwood, was awarded the George Medal for his part in rescuing Swiss F1 driver

Clay Regazzoni from his burning BRM during the 1973 South African Grand Prix.

On lap three of the race, Hailwood's Surtees had a minor collision with the Lotus of Dave Charlton, as a result of which Hailwood's car went into a spin and was collected by Regazzoni's BRM.

The force of the impact rendered the Swiss driver unconscious and caused his BRM to catch fire. Seeing that Regazzoni had been knocked out, Hailwood braved the flames, undid Regazzoni's safety belts and attempted to pull him out of the blazing BRM. In the process, his own racing overalls caught fire, causing him to have to temporarily break off his rescue attempt.

Hailwood then returned to the BRM and, with the aid of a marshal, succeeded in pulling Regazzoni to safety. That Regazzoni escaped serious injury was largely due to Hailwood's courage.

Former paratrooper David Purley found himself in a similar situation at the Dutch Grand Prix later that season, when he attempted to rescue Roger Williamson from his burning, upside-down March.

A tyre had failed on Williamson's car, causing it to strike the armco at high speed, flip over and catch fire. Purley, who was not involved in the accident, stopped his own car and, in the absence of suitably equipped marshals, made repeated efforts to rescue the stricken Williamson. Tragically, Purley's heroic actions were in vain, and Williamson perished.

Four years later, Purley was himself involved in a serious accident when the throttle of his LEC struck open in qualifying for the British Grand Prix. The car hit a wall and decelerated from 108 mph to a standstill in the space of twenty-six inches. Remarkably, Purley survived the accident, the force of which was estimated at 179.8 g, albeit with severe injuries to his legs, pelvis and ribs. He recovered and raced again.

In a macabre twist of fate, both Hailwood and Purley died in accidents at the age of 40: Hailwood in 1981, and Purley in 1985.

D16

Who is the only one of the following drivers to have driven for Williams in the season after winning the world championship with them?

C.   Jacques Villeneuve

Of the seven drivers who have won the World Drivers' Championship in a Williams, only three of them remained with the team to defend their title: Alan Jones (champion in 1980), Keke Rosberg (champion in 1982), and Jacques Villeneuve (champion in 1997).

Those who left the team after winning the title are: Nelson Piquet (champion in 1987, went to Lotus for 1988), Nigel Mansell (champion in 1992, went to race in the USA), Alain Prost (champion in 1993, retired), and Damon Hill (champion in 1996, went to Arrows).

Williams is the only F1 team to have world champions in two successive years (Mansell and Prost) leave the team without defending their title.

Although five of the aforementioned seven drivers went on to win further Grands Prix (Villeneuve and Prost being the exceptions), no-one who won a world championship for Williams has ever won another championship after leaving the team, a curious fact that's true of only one other team: Brawn, for whom Jenson Button won his sole world title in the only year in which the team competed.

D17

How many times was Stirling Moss runner-up in the world championship?

B.   Four

Stirling Moss finished second in the F1 world championship for four consecutive years, from 1955 to 1958. He lost out a single point in 1958 and by three in 1956.

He followed his string of runner-up spots with three straight third place finishes in the championship standings between 1959 and 1961, but retired from the sport in 1962 after crashing heavily in a non-championship race at Goodwood.

Eighteen years later, he returned to regular competition when he partnered Martin Brundle in the Audi team in the 1980 British Saloon Car Championship.

Throughout his career, Moss demonstrated great versatility in addition to his very considerable ability: he finished second in the 1952 Monte Carlo Rally, was twice second in the Le Mans 24 Hours, won both the Sebring and Reims 12 Hours and won the 1955 Mille Miglia in a record time.

He passed away in April, 2020, at the age of 90.

D18

In what year did David Coulthard's spin trigger a first lap pile-up at Spa?

A. 1998

The 1998 Belgian Grand Prix was memorable for three reasons: a first lap multiple car pile-up on the run down to Eau Rouge as a result of David Coulthard's spin; Damon Hill taking Jordan's first (and his last) Grand Prix win, with team-mate Ralf Schumacher second; and the collision between Coulthard and Michael Schumacher that that ended the German's race and dented his championship aspirations.

The race started in very wet conditions, with Coulthard making a poor start from his front row grid slot. He compounded this by running wide on the exit of the La Source hairpin and losing control of his McLaren, which speared across the track into the armco and thereafter rebounded into the path of oncoming cars. All hell then broke loose, with a total of thirteen cars sustaining damage to some degree.

The race restarted from scratch over an hour later, with four cars absent. After 24 laps Michael Schumacher had built up a sizeable lead and was coming up to lap Coulthard's McLaren. Having been instructed to allow Schumacher past, Coulthard slowed but stayed on the racing line. Schumacher, unsighted by the spray, expected Coulthard to have moved off-line and consequently drove into the back of him, thereby ending his race.

An irate Schumacher subsequently attempted to accost Coulthard in the pits, accusing the Scot of having tried to kill him. Amid the chaos and recriminations, Damon Hill led team-mate Ralf Schumacher home to score Jordan's first Grand Prix victory.

Coulthard put his 1998 nightmare behind him the following year, when he led Hakkinen home in a 1-2 finish for McLaren.

D19

How many Grands Prix did Eddie Irvine win at Ferrari?

A.   Four

Eddie Irvine won four Grands Prix in his career. They all came in 1999, the year in which his Ferrari team-mate Michael Schumacher was sidelined for several races after breaking his right leg in the British Grand Prix.

Three of Irvine's wins came after Schumacher's accident and two of them – the German and Malaysian Grands Prix – were effectively gifted to Irvine by his team-mates (Mika Salo in Germany, Michael Schumacher in Malaysia).

Those four wins, plus a series of errors and misfortunes that befell reigning world champion Mika Hakkinen, saw Irvine sit at the top of the championship standings going the final race of the season at Suzuka. For Irvine, the equation was simple: he would be champion provided that Hakkinen scored fewer than four points more than him in the race.

This meant that Hakkinen would be champion if he won the race, but if Schumacher were to win with Hakkinen second then Irvine could afford to come in fourth and still take the title. Motorsport fans across the globe looked forward to what promised to be an epic title shoot-out.

As it turned out, however, neither Ferrari driver was able to mount a serious challenge to the Finn, who won the race and therefore retained the world championship.

It was Irvine's last race for Ferrari. Never again would he win a Grand Prix let alone come within touching distance of the world championship. Indeed, the best that he could muster in three seasons with the Jaguar team was a brace of third place finishes. He left F1 at the end of the 2002 season.

D20

Who was the last Italian driver to win a Grand Prix for Ferrari?

B. Michele Alboreto

As at May, 2020, fifteen Italian drivers have won one or more Grands Prix. Of that number, eight tasted victory at the wheel of a Ferrari: Alboreto, Ascari, Baghetti, Bandini, Farina, Musso, Scarfiotti and Taruffi.

Between them, they won a total of twenty-two Grands Prix for Ferrari as a constructor (Baghetti's sole win was at the wheel of a privately entered Ferrari), with Ascari contributing thirteen of those wins, and Alboreto taking three.

Since 1992, only two Italians – Giancarlo Fisichella and Luca Badoer – have raced for Ferrari in F1, both of them in 2009 as temporary stand-ins for the injured Felipe Massa.

The Teams I

T1

In what year did Honda's 'Earth car' livery appear?

A.   2007

The Honda RA107 F1 car featured a unique livery – depicting the planet Earth against the void of space - that, said Honda, reflected the company's concern for the environment.

Apart from the Honda 'H', the only other logo to appear on the car was that of Bridgestone, who supplied tyres to all the F1 teams.

Unfortunately, the RA107's livery was the best thing about it. Jenson Button and Rubens Barrichello did their best, but so dire was the car that the team only scored six points all season, all of which were scored by Jenson Button.

T2

Eddie Jordan sold his F1 in team in 2005. Under which name did the team start the 2006 season?

D.   Midland

The team was purchased from Eddie Jordan by Russo-Canadian businessman, Alex Shnaider, and re-registered as Midland F1 Racing.

It ran under that banner for the first fifteen Grands Prix of the 2006 season before changing its name to 'Spyker MF1 Racing', the team having been sold by Shnaider to Spyker Cars N.V., a Dutch sports car manufacturer.

Another change of name, to Spyker F1, followed before the start of the 2007 season. The team was, however, sold again that season to a consortium led by Indian businessman Vijay Mallya. Another change of name followed, and it contested the 2008 season as Force India.

Following further changes in ownership, it currently competes as Racing Point, but from 2021 it will race as Aston Martin.

T3

Which of these F1 teams used their own W12 engine?

B.   Life

The Life F1 team came about when Italian businessman Ernesto Vita bought the rights to a new 3.5 litre engine designed by ex-Ferrari engineer, Franco Rocchi.

Rocchi's engine was unusual in that it featured three banks of four cylinders, with the result that it was as short as a V8 engine but quite a bit taller.

The engine came into being at a time when turbochargers had been outlawed from F1, and many of the teams were in the market for normally aspirated units. Vita therefore bought the rights to the engine in the hope that he would be able to supply it to an existing F1 team. But when no takers came forward, he decided to form his own F1 team: Life Racing.

Life purchased a chassis from First Racing, who had intended to use it themselves in the 1989 F1 championship but withdrew their entry before the season started. Now known as the Life L190, the car was married up to the W12 engine under the direction of another ex-Ferrari man, Gianni Marelli.

From the outside, the picture was completed when Gary Brabham, son of three times world champion, Jack, was signed up to race the L190.

The team was, however, woefully ill-equipped to compete in F1. At the start of the season it had one chassis, one engine (which delivered at least 120 bhp less than any other F1 engine used that season) and few spares. The L190 was underpowered, overweight and top-heavy. It was pitifully lacking in straightline speed, grip and balance.

And if that wasn't enough of a challenge for Brabham, the Life mechanics went on strike in Brazil. When Brabham took the L190 out onto the circuit, its engine seized after about 400 metres. The cause soon became apparent: the disgruntled mechanics hadn't put any oil in it! Brabham wisely left the team shortly thereafter.

His place was taken by former Alfa Romeo F1 driver Bruno Giacomelli. Unfortunately, Giacomelli's efforts were wasted on the L190. The car was both appallingly slow and extremely unreliable. Like Brabham, Giacomelli was never able to get it through pre-qualifying.

The team replaced the W12 with a Judd V8 for the Portuguese and Spanish Grands Prix, but this made no appreciable difference to the performance of the car. In Portugal, the engine cover, which hadn't been modified when the engines were swapped, flew off on the car's first lap around the track, bringing its participation to an end.

The Judd-powered Life did at least take part in pre-qualifying for the Spanish Grand Prix, but Giacomelli's best lap was nearly twenty-four seconds slower than Senna's pole position time. The team folded after Spain and did not see out the season.

As for the other teams mentioned, neither Kauhsen nor Andrea Moda's cars ever qualified for a Grand Prix. Maki did manage to do so once, when the number of available race slots exceeded the number of entrants, but their only engine blew up before the race.

T4

What engines did Williams use during the 1988 season?

A.   Judd

Having lost engine supplier Honda to McLaren, Williams went into the 1988 season without a turbocharged engine. Although they had inked a deal with Renault to supply normally aspirated engines, this wouldn't take effect until 1989.

For the 1988 season, Williams therefore struck a deal with British engine supplier, Judd. It proved to be a tough season, however, for everyone except McLaren, who used their Honda engines to win all but one of the season's sixteen Grands Prix.

As for Williams, the best that they could muster was a brace of second places for Nigel Mansell, who retired from twelve of the other fourteen rounds and missed the remaining two due to illness.

T5

Which team was purchased by Benetton in 1985?

C.   Toleman

Founded by haulage mogul Ted Toleman in 1977, Toleman Motorsport first tasted success in Formula 2 (winning the championship in 1980) before entering Formula 1 in 1981.

Using a turbocharged engine designed and built by Hart, it took the team some time to find its feet in F1. A fairly disastrous 1981 season, in which drivers Derek Warwick and Brian Henton each managed to qualify for only one race out of the twelve contested by them, was followed by a better, but still pointless, season in 1982. The team's fortunes changed somewhat in 1983, however, when Warwick reeled off a string of good finishes towards the end of the season.

The 1984 season marked the high-water mark of the team's time in F1, with new boy Ayrton Senna scoring three podium finishes, including a second place at Monaco. Unfortunately for Toleman, Senna left the team at the end of the season in favour of a drive with Team Lotus.

Tyre supply issues meant that the team missed the first three Grands Prix of 1985, resulting in the team losing Senna's intended replacement, Stefan Johansson, to Ferrari. Matters thereafter improved, with Benetton coming on board as the main sponsor and Teo Fabi taking the team's first (and only) pole position at the German Grand Prix. That was as good as it got, however, and the team failed to score a championship point that season.

Benetton purchased the team in the off-season and renamed the team accordingly. They continued to race in F1, winning two world championships with Michael Schumacher in 1994 and 1995, before being purchased by Renault in 1999.

As Renault, the team won two further championships, with Fernando Alonso, in 2005 and 2006. It was then sold to Genii Capital and competed first as Lotus Renault GP and then as Lotus F1 Team between 2011 and 2015 before being re-acquired by Renault.

T6

Which F1 team was owned by Bernie Ecclestone?

B.   Brabham

Founded by Jack Brabham and Ron Tauranac, Motor Racing Developments Limited (to use the company's full legal name) was run by the two men throughout the sixties.

The cars produced by the company initially bore the name 'MRD' but this was soon changed to Brabham. Although the company's racing cars competed with much success at various levels of motorsport, their biggest triumphs came in F1, with Jack Brabham winning the world championship in 1966 and team-mate Denny Hulme taking the honours the following year.

As the 1960s came to an end, Jack Brabham decided to retire and return home to Australia(although he ended up postponing this for a year). He therefore sold his share in the company to Ron Tauranac.

A further change followed in 1971, when Tauranac, more comfortable as an engineer than a businessman, sold the company to Bernie Ecclestone. Under Ecclestone's stewardship, Brabham won several Grands Prix in the 1970s before hitting a purple patch in the early 1980s, with Nelson Piquet taking the world championship in both 1981 and 1983.

As the 1980s wore on, however, Ecclestone's focus was increasingly on his role with the Formula One Constructor's Association rather than his F1 team. The team's performance slipped and slipped again, and in 1986 it could only muster a total of two points in that year's world championship.

The following season was a little better, but with engine supplier BMW having decided to leave the sport, Brabham struggled to find a new source of engines. The team did not compete in the 1988 F1 world championship and was sold by Ecclestone that year.

Brabham returned to F1 under new ownership in 1989. It was then sold again and continued to race on, with ever-deteriorating results, until folding during the 1992 season.

T7

Which of these world champions did NOT race for his own F1 team?

B.   Jackie Stewart

Although Jackie Stewart tested various Formula One cars in the years following his retirement from racing in 1973, he never returned to competitive racing.

His return to F1 as chairman of the Stewart F1 team came about through his son, Paul Stewart, who had started his own racing team in the late 1980s. Paul Stewart Racing, as the team was then known, competed in various categories of the sport from 1989 onwards, enjoying considerable success.

The move into Formula One was facilitated by a five-year deal with Ford, with whom Jackie Stewart had long been associated. The first fruits of that association were seen in 1997, when the first Stewart Grand Prix car, the SF01, took second place in the rain-hit Monaco Grand Prix.

That apart, results were hard to come by during the first two years of the team's existence. The situation improved markedly in 1999, however, with Rubens Barrichello taking three third places and Johnny Herbert scoring the team's first (and only) win in tricky conditions at the European Grand Prix. Those results were sufficient to elevate the team to fourth place in the constructors' championship.

With the team's fortunes on the up, Ford made the Stewarts a financial offer they couldn't refuse in the winter of 1999. The team was then rebranded as Jaguar Racing, It competed in that guise until the end of the 2004 season, amassing only two podium finishes in that time.

Towards the end of 2004, Ford struck a deal to sell the team to drinks company Red Bull. The team was promptly renamed Red Bull Racing. And the rest is, as they say, history...

T8

Which team was the first to win fifty Grands Prix?

C.   Lotus

In spite of not having entered Formula One until 1958, Team Lotus was the first team to win 50 Grands Prix.

Having taken its first win at the 1961 United States Grand Prix, Team Lotus racked up its fiftieth victory when Ronnie Peterson won at Monaco in 1974.

Half of those victories were taken by one man: Jim Clark, with Ronnie Peterson and Emerson Fittipaldi the next highest contributors on nine wins apiece.

Ferrari was the second team to reach the half century of Grand Prix wins, reaching the mark just five races later, albeit having competed in appreciably more Grands Prix than the Hethel outfit.

Lotus was also the first *constructor* to win fifty Grands Prix, a feat it achieved in 1973 thanks to Rob Walker's privately-run Lotuses having taken five Grand Prix victories between 1960 and 1968.

T9

Who scored the first Grand Priz victory for Williams?

A.   Clay Regazzoni

Frank Williams had been entering cars in Grands Prix for almost a decade when he founded Williams Grand Prix Engineering in 1977.

That season, the team ran a March 761 for Belgian driver Patrick Nève. For 1978, however, the team fielded its own car, the FW06, designed by Patrick Head and driven by Alan Jones. It performed reasonably well, taking second place in the United States (East) Grand Prix.

For 1979, the team entered two cars, Jones being joined by former Ferrari driver Clay Regazzoni. A new car, the ground-effect FW07, designed by Head and featuring the work of aerodynamicist Frank Dernie, made its debut in the fifth round of the championship. It wasn't a winner straight out of the box, but it clearly had potential – potential that was realised at the British Grand Prix.

Jones simply obliterated the rest of the field in qualifying at Silverstone and was on his way to a comfortable victory when his engine failed. That left Regazzoni to win the race, well ahead of René Arnoux in a Renault. Jones then went on a run of three victories on the trot and later added a fourth.

Partnered by new team-mate Carlos Reutemann, the Australian took the 1980 world championship with relative ease, thus becoming the first driver to win the world championship in a Williams.

T10

Which was the only team to race a gas turbine-powered car in F1?

D.   Lotus

Given their track record of motorsport innovation, it shouldn't really come as a surprise to learn that Lotus was the first – and so far only – constructor to race a gas turbine car in F1.

That car, the 56B, was a development of the all-wheel-drive, Pratt & Whitney powered Type 56 in which Art Leonard had come desperately close to winning the Indianapolis 500 in 1968.

With gas turbines thereafter effectively being banned from IndyCar racing,

Lotus adapted the Type 56 for Formula One. The resulting Lotus 56B took part in three Grands Prix in 1971. It was, however, too heavy (the engine's fuel consumption meant that larger fuel tanks had to be fitted, adding weight), and its lack of engine braking and slow throttle response were hardly ideal for F1.

It only finished one of the three Grands Prix in which it ran, Emerson Fittipaldi taking it to eighth place in Italy. After a final outing in a Formula 5000 race in Germany, in which it finished second with Fittipaldi at the wheel, it was quietly retired by Lotus.

The Teams II

T11

In which year did Williams last win a Grand Prix?

A.   2012

Although Williams have taken 114 Grand Prix victories, only eleven of those have come in the 21st century, and just one in the last sixteen years.

That sole win since 2004 was taken by Pastor Maldonado at the 2012 Spanish Grand Prix. It was Maldonado's first – and so far only – Grand Prix victory.

In winning at Barcelona, Maldonado became a member of an exclusive club of drivers - Giancarlo Baghetti, Jo Bonnier, Vittorio Brambilla, Peter Gethin, and Ludovico Scarfiotti – to have won one Grand Prix but never otherwise finished in a podium position.

T12

Which of the following F1 Team Principals also raced in a Grand Prix?

A.   Gerrard Larrousse

As a driver, Gerrard Larrousse is best known for his exploits in rallying, in which he won the 1969 Tour De Corse and was second in the Monte Carlo Rally on three occasions, and sportscar racing, in which he won the Sebring 12 Hours, the Nürburgring 1000 kilometres and, on two occasions, the Le Mans 24 Hours.

He did, however, race in the 1974 Belgian Grand Prix, for which he qualified in a very respectable eleventh position. He entered one more Grand Prix, the 1974 French Grand Prix, but was one of eight drivers who failed to qualify.

Larrousse went on to manage the Renault F1 team before founding an eponymous Formula One team. The team competed from 1987 to 1994, but largely struggled at a time when as many as twenty-one different teams took part in the championship.

Bernie Ecclestone entered two Grands Prix in 1958, but raced in neither of them.

Colin Chapman took part in qualifying for the 1956 French Grand Prix for the Vanwall team, but was unable to start the race after damaging his car in a collision with Van wall team-mate, Mike Hawthorn.

It's often stated that Chapman qualified in fifth position for the race, but a contemporary report states that Chapman's best qualifying time was actually set not by him but by another of his team-mates, Harry Schell. As the time was set in Chapman's car, which bore his race number, it was credited to him.

Christian Horner raced in Formula 3000. He did not enjoy great success as a driver but the team he founded, Arden, has been highly successful.

T13

Who won the first Grand Prix for McLaren as a constructor?

C.   Bruce McLaren

Bruce McLaren didn't just found the team that bears his name; he also took its first wins in both F1 and the Can-Am Championship.

Having competed in F1 since 1966, the team's first Grand Prix win came when McLaren took the Ford DFV-powered M7A to victory in the 1968 Belgian Grand Prix at Spa-Francorchamps. His team-mate, reigning world champion Denny Hulme, thereafter took two further wins for the team that season, in Italy and Canada.

That victory in Belgium would turn out to be Bruce McLaren's final Grand Prix win. The team he formed would, however, go on to win two World Drivers' Championships and one Constructors' Championship in the 1970s before being acquired by Ron Dennis's Project 4 organisation in 1980.

T14

What engine did McLaren test, but not use in a Grand Prix, in 1993?

A.   Lamborghini

Following Honda's withdrawal from F1 at the end of 1992, McLaren had been unable to secure a supply of 'works' engines for the 1993 season.

The result was a season in which they attempted to compete with the dominant Williams using a car powered by a customer-specification Ford V8 engine. The Ford engine was tractable and reliable but even in works specification it gave away over 50 bhp to the Renault V10 used by Williams.

Something more powerful was therefore needed, which is where the Lamborghini V12 came in. Designed by former Ferrari designer, Mauro Forghieri, the Lamborghini V12 had been around since 1989 but had never been used by one of the top F1 teams. With both McLaren and Lamborghini in search of suitable partners, it made sense for the two of them to hook up.

A deal was therefore struck whereby McLaren would modify one of their current F1 cars to test the Lamborghini engine. These tests duly took place at Estoril and Silverstone during the latter part of the 1993 season.

Ayrton Senna and Mika Hakkinen both drove the Lamborghini-powered car and were impressed by not only the engine but also by the handling of the modified MP4/8 chassis. Indeed, Hakkinen lapped Silverstone over a second faster than in the Ford-powered car in back to back tests.

That was, however, as far as the project went. With McLaren having signed a deal with Peugeot for the 1994 season, the plug was pulled on the Lamborghini V12 engine project and it disappeared from F1 at the end of the 1993 season.

T15

Who succeeded Stefano Domenicali as the Team Principal of Scuderia

Ferrari?

B.   Marco Mattiacci

Mattiacci's reign as Team Principal of Scuderia Ferrari was a short one: just 8 months.

Having taken over from Stefano Domenicali after the Scuderia made a poor start to the 2014 season, Mattiacci had the misfortune to preside over the team's worst season since the early 1990s, with the red cars failing to amass even a single Grand Prix victory.

Although his time in charge was brief, he nonetheless oversaw the departure of Fernando Alonso from the team, the hiring of Sebastian Vettel and the laying of the foundations for a somewhat more successful 2015 season.

Mattiaci's replacement, Mauricio Arrivabene, lasted for four seasons in the role. But with both the Drivers' and Constructors' Championships continuing to elude the Scuderia, he was replaced in January 2019 by Mattia Binotto.

T16

For which team did Ron Dennis first work in F1?

D.   Cooper

Ron Dennis's rise to the pinnacle of motorsport management began in 1966, when at the age of 18 he joined the Cooper F1 team as a mechanic.

When Cooper's star driver Jochen Rindt moved to Brabham in 1968, Dennis moved with him. He stayed there until 1971, when he and Neil Trundle formed their own team, Rondel Racing.

Dennis followed this up by forming two new teams: Project Three Racing in the mid-1970s, and Project Four Racing in the late 1970s.

Success followed success, and in 1980 Dennis's Project Four operation took over the ailing McLaren Formula One team.

Four years later, McLaren scooped both the Drivers' and Constructors' World Championships – the first of many successes (including four consecutive Drivers' and Constructors' World Championships) under Dennis's stewardship.

T17

The ATS team that competed in F1 from 1977 to 1984 shared its acronym with a previous F1 team from which country?

A.   Italy

Gunther Schmidt, the owner of *Auto Technisches Spezialzubehör* (better known as ATS Wheels), formed the ATS F1 team in 1977 as a way of promoting the company and its products. The team ran a year-old Penske chassis that year but thereafter developed its own chassis.

A number of talented drivers drove for ATS over the years, including Keke Rosberg, Gerhard Berger, Jean-Pierre Jarier, Jochen Mass, Hans-Joachim Stuck and Manfred Winkelhock. But in spite of this, success proved to be elusive, and the team only scored a total of five points finishes (points then being awarded down to only sixth place) in the 101 Grands Prix which it entered.

The team folded at the end of the 1984 season, after which Schmidt left the company. He thereafter purchased another wheel manufacturer, Rial, and formed a new F1 team under that banner in 1988. It lasted for two seasons, scoring two fourth place finishes in that time. Both Rial and ATS continue to manufacture wheels to this day.

The original ATS team – *Automobili Turismo e Sport* – was formed in Italy in :1961 by a number of former Ferrari employees, including Carlo Chiti and Giotto Bizzarrini.

ATS was created with the intention of rivalling Ferrari both as a racing team and as producer of sports cars for the road. It succeeded in neither ambition. Although it built its own F1 car and 1.5 litre engine, its F1 team contested just five Grands Prix, all in 1963. Its sole road car, the pretty, mid-engined ATS 2500 GT, fared no better and was built only in very limited numbers.

ATS's F1 engine did, however, outlast the team: it was used by the Derrington-Francis team in one Grand Prix in 1964 before making a final appearance, in 2.7 litre form, in Silvio Moser's Cooper in 1967.

T18

In which decade did Scuderia Ferrari win the most Grands Prix?

D.   2000s

Of the two hundred and thirty-eight Grands Prix won by Ferrari as a constructor, no fewer than eighty-five of those victories came in a single decade: from 2000 to 2009.

The Scuderia enjoyed a sustained period of dominance between 2000 and 2004, scoring fifty-seven Grand Prix victories in just five seasons. It found the going much tougher in 2005, however, winning just one Grand Prix - the 2005 US Grand Prix, in which only six cars competed.

It bounced back and took another twenty-six wins from 2006 to 2008, but the decade ended in disappointment, with Kimi Raikkonen notching the team's only victory in the 2009 season.

Prior to the 2000s, Ferrari's most successful decade had been the 1970s, in which it took thirty-seven Grand Prix wins to go with three World Drivers' Championships and four Constructors' Championships.

There was no such thing as the Constructors' Championship in the 1950s, but Ferrari drivers took the world championship four times in that decade, scoring twenty-nine wins in the process – a number that looks a lot more impressive when measured against the number of Grands Prix run in that era.

Outside of those three decades, success has been much more elusive, with only two Drivers' World Championships (Phil Hill in 1961 and John

Surtees in 1964) and five Constructors' Championships (1961, 1964, 1982, 1983 and 1999) having fallen to the Scuderia across four decades of racing.

As it stands, Ferrari has won nothing in terms of championships since taking the Constructors' Championship in 2008. And with the team's 2020 challenger having being somewhat off the pace, Ferrari's wait for a championship trophy will continue for a little longer.

T19

Which Grand Prix-winning team beseeched The Great Chicken in the Sky to supply them with a replacement engine?

B.   Hesketh

During their brief time in Formula One, the Hesketh team became known for the entertaining way in which they went about their business, which included the team manager selling the team owner's Rolls-Royce, without asking for his permission, so that the team could soldier on. And they did, to great effect during the two and a half seasons that James Hunt drove for them in F1.

Their greatest eccentricity may, however, have been their habit of gathering in a circle and clucking to The Great Chicken in the Sky. But laugh not, for this ritual bore fruit on at least one notable occasion.

Having entered a Surtees F1 car for James Hunt at the 1973 Race of Champions at Brands Hatch, the team's only DFV engine expired. This was the cue for a multitude of team members to form a circle in the paddock and make clucking noises. When Max Mosley of the March team asked what they were doing, he was told that they were asking The Great Chicken in the Sky to supply them with another engine.

Mosley arranged to loan them one of the March team's engines, which Hunt made good use of by finishing third in the race. Mosley's generosity was not forgotten by Hunt, who thereafter called him "The Great Chicken of Bicester".

There was more to the Hesketh team than madcap antics, though, as evidenced by the nine podiums it achieved between 1973 and 1975, including a magnificent win at the 1975 Dutch Grand Prix when James Hunt beat Ferrari's world champion-elect, Niki Lauda, in a straight fight.

But like all good parties, it couldn't last forever: the end of the 1975 season saw Lord Hesketh withdraw from Hesketh Racing, James Hunt head off to McLaren and designer Harvey Postlethwaite join the Wolf-Williams team. Hesketh Racing soldiered on under the stewardship of Bubbles Horsley for a while, but it was a losing battle and the team finally folded during the 1978 season.

T20

Which constructor won every Grand Prix in 1950?

C.   Alfa Romeo

The Milanese team utterly dominated Formula 1's inaugural season, with Nino Farina and Juan Manuel Fangio each winning three Grands Prix on their way to first and second in the Drivers' Championship.

The only other driver to win a round of the F1 world championship was Johnnie Parsons of the USA, who took victory in the Indianapolis 500 at the wheel of a Kurtis Kraft with an Offenhauser engine. Indianapolis was, however, run to different rules than the other rounds of the world championship and was therefore not regarded as a Grand Prix.

Surely Not I

S1

Why did David Coulthard retire from the 1995 Australian GP?

A.   He crashed at the pit lane entrance

David Coulthard's first full season of F1 had both its ups and downs. Winning the Portuguese Grand Prix from pole position was definitely one of the former, but this was balanced out by a couple of very public faux pas towards the end of the season.

The first of his blunders came in Italy, where, having taken pole position, he contrived to spin off on the formation lap. His luck was in, though, as a first lap pile-up that caused the race to be re-started gave him a second bite at the cherry, albeit in the team's spare car. He led the race from the restart until a failed wheel bearing put him out after 13 laps.

Gaffe number two came in the season-ending Grand Prix. Having taken the lead at the start, Coulthard seemed to be in prime position to double his total of Grand Prix victories for the season. Until he pulled off the circuit to make a scheduled pit stop, that is.

Having carried too much speed into the pitlane access road, he braked a little too hard on the approach to the right hand bend that led into the pitlane. His front wheels locked and he slid into the armco and out of the race.

Ah well, they do say that the best lessons are the ones that are hardest learned, and DC learned enough to win twelve more Grands Prix in an F1 career that lasted for a further thirteen years.

Oh, and if you're thinking that an exploding fire extinguisher is the sort of thing that only happens in fiction then think again, for it happened to Mario Andretti in practice for the 1977 Argentinian Grand Prix. Mario was lucky to escape with bruised legs when the nose-mounted fire extinguisher in his Lotus 78 went bang, the car itself being so badly damaged that it had to be flown back to the UK for repairs.

Who protested about the 7.45 a.m. start of the warm-up session for the 1984 Dallas Grand Prix by turning up in his pyjamas?

B.   Jacques Laffite

Holding a Grand Prix in Texas in the heat of July must have seemed like a good idea at the time. Unfortunately, the merits (and there were quite a few) of the track laid out in the Texas State Fair Grounds in Dallas were undone by a surface that quite literally fell apart in the blazing heat – at one point, the track temperature was measured at 66 degrees Centigrade. The upshot of this was that the track surface soon looked more like a gravel rally stage than an F1 circuit.

There was talk of cancelling the race but in the end it was decided to move the race forward to 11.00 am, three hours earlier than scheduled. This meant that the 30 minute morning warm-up session that preceded a Grand Prix in those days was also brought forward to 7.45 am, a move that caused Jacques Laffite to protest by turning up at the circuit in his pyjamas. As it turned out, however, the warm-up was cancelled due to the ongoing attempts to make the track surface fit for racing.

When the race eventually started, car after car dropped out, leaving Williams' Keke Rosberg to take the first Grand Prix win for the turbocharged Honda engine.

Rosberg had cannily worn a special water-cooled skullcap to help him cope with the fierce heat whereas others, such as Osella's Piercarlo Ghinzani, resorted to less sophisticated means of keeping cool – in Ghinzani's case this involved his pit crew throwing a bucket of water over him at a pit stop.

The race was also notable for Nigel Mansell's attempt to push his stricken Lotus over the finishing line, an effort that saw him pass out due to heat exhaustion.

The Dallas Grand Prix never again featured in the F1 calendar. A pity, as it could have made for a good addition to the championship had it been held at a cooler time of year.

S3

How did Harry Schell qualify on the front row of the grid for the 1959 United States Grand Prix?

B.   He took a shortcut

It's inconceivable to modern eyes, but Harry Schell successfully improved his lap time and grid position by taking a shortcut!

Although the shortcut taken by Schell cut out a significant portion (perhaps as much as 1/3rd) of the 5.2 mile circuit, he did not avail himself of it until he was sure that no race officials were watching him. Even so, he shaved about six seconds off his previous best time of 3 minutes 11.2 seconds.

In spite of protests led by the Ferrari team, Schell was permitted to start from his front-row grid slot. His opportunism didn't help him in the race, however, as he retired after just five laps.

The race was won by Bruce McLaren, who thereby became the (then) youngest-ever Grand Prix winner. Moreover, Jack Brabham's fourth place (he had to push the car over the line after running out of fuel) ensured that not only did he become the first Australian world champion but also that the Cooper driven by him became the first rear-engined car to win the F1 world championship.

A race of firsts, then, but it also turned out to be the last Grand Prix for nearly sixty years in which a point was awarded for fastest lap.

S4

Which F1 driver was kidnapped in Cuba in 1958?

B.   Juan Manuel Fangio

First held in 1957, the Cuban Grand Prix was a sports car race run on a street circuit in Havana.

The 1957 race, won by Juan Manuel Fangio in a Maserati 300S from Carroll Shelby and Fon De Portago in Ferraris, was a great success. So, even though revolution (against the regime of Cuban President Batiista) was in the air, it was run again in 1958. Maserati sent a strong team which included both Fangio and Stirling Moss. This time, however, Fangio failed to make the start of the race let alone the finish.

The night before the race, two men armed with guns kidnapped Fangio from his hotel in Havana and took him to a house. As the police tried (without success) to find Fangio, President Batista insisted that the race should go ahead as planned.

Tragically, it ended in disaster after only six laps, the Ferrari driven by Armando Cifuentes having left the track and gone into the crowd due to oil on the surface. Seven people were killed.

Fangio, who had been well treated by his captors, was released unharmed a few hours later. The kidnappers were hostile to Batista's regime and had hoped that kidnapping Fangio would cause the race to be cancelled. As it was, Batista was overthrown on 1st January, 1959.

S5

Apart from Alberto Ascari, which other driver has crashed into the harbour during the Monaco Grand Prix?

C.   Paul Hawkins

In 1965, a decade after Ascari and his Lancia D50 ended up in Monte Carlo's harbour, Australian driver Paul Hawkins inadvertently took his Lotus 33 for a swim. Like Ascari, Hawkins was none the worse for the experience, although the same couldn't be said for either his Lotus or Ascari's Lancia when they were fished out of the water.

Hawkins only had a brief dalliance with F1, racing in just three Grands Prix, but had a longer and much more successful career as a sports car racer, winning the Targa Florio, Paris 1000 km and Zeltweg 500 km races in 1967. He enjoyed further success in 1968, winning the Monza 1000 km, finishing second in the Watkins Glen 6 Hours and scoring third places in both the Nurburgring 1000 km and Zeltweg 500 km races.

S6

Who crashed heavily in the 2003 Brazilian GP yet finished third?

C.   Fernando Alonso

The first nine laps, of a scheduled seventy-one, were run behind the pace car. What followed thereafter was a race that that had pretty much everything: daring overtaking manoeuvres, more spins than a tumble dryer, an on-track 'river' that claimed multiple victims including Michael Schumacher, and a winner that wasn't. Oh, and the Safety Car was deployed a total of five times during the race.

McLaren team-mates Coulthard and Raikkonen, Ferrari's Barrichello and Jordan's Fisichella all led the race at different stages. But as the race entered its final quarter, it seemed that Coulthard, then lying third, held all the aces, given that he was the only one of the leading drivers who didn't need to stop again for fuel before the end of the race.

But if DC thought that victory would soon be his, he was mistaken. On lap 54, Mark Webber lost control of his Jaguar on the long left-hand curve that leads onto the pit straight. The Australian was unhurt but debris from his car, including three of its wheels, was strewn across the circuit.

The Safety car was deployed and the marshals frantically waved yellow flags to alert drivers to the danger ahead. Unfortunately, Fernando Alonso, who was running in fourth place after an eventful race that had seen him make an extra pit stop for tyres as well as receive a stop-go penalty for overtaking under a yellow flag, was discussing tyre selection on his car-pit radio and missed the waved yellows. The result was that his Renault ploughed into one of the stray wheels from Webber's Jaguar, causing it to hit a tyre wall then rebound across the track and slam into a concrete barrier.

With debris littering the track and medical personnel tending to the injured

Alonso, the race was red flagged on lap 56 and Raikkonen declared to be the winner from Fisichella and Alonso, who was then on his way to hospital. A frustrated Coulthard was fourth.

A few days later, it emerged that the race officials hadn't realised that Fisichella had already started his 56th lap when the race was stopped. This error meant that they had based the results on the race order as at the end of lap 53 rather than lap 54. As Fischella had passed Raikkonen for the lead on lap 54, he was the race winner. The official results were duly amended and Fisichella was presented with the winner's trophy before the next Grand Prix on the calendar. Alonso remained third and Coulthard, no doubt still frustrated, remained fourth.

It was Fisichella's first Grand Prix victory as well as being the last for both Ford (as an engine supplier) and the Jordan Grand Prix team.

S7

What happened to Taki Inoue at the 1995 Hungarian Grand Prix?

B.   He was run over by a course car

Taki Inoue raced in just eighteen Grands Prix (one for Simtek in 1994, the other seventeen for Footwork in 1995), but in spite of failing to score a world championship point he nonetheless claimed his place in F1 lore.

Inoue's claim to undying infamy came at the 1995 Hungarian Grand Prix. After his Footwork stopped out on the circuit with an engine problem, Inoue was leading a marshal with a fire extinguisher across the grass verge towards his stricken car when both he and the marshal were hit by a course car.

Bizarrely, it was Inoue's second unfortunate encounter with a course car that season: his Footwork, with him in it, was being towed back to the pits at Monaco when it was hit by a course car driven by French rally ace Jean Ragnotti.

Inoue left Formula One at the end of 1995 and hung up his crash helmet in 1999. Today, he looks back on the incidents which attended his brief F1

278

career with self-deprecating good humour.

S8

Which driver punched a marshal after crashing out of the 1977 Canadian Grand Prix?

A.   James Hunt

This is really two 'surely not' moments in the same question. The first came when Hunt, who had just passed Mario Andretti for the lead of the race, ran into the back of McLaren team-mate Jochen Mass, who was then in third place, whilst attempting to lap him.

Mass was able to continue, but Hunt's McLaren was too badly damaged to even make it back round to the pits. A furious Hunt, who blamed Mass for costing him the race win, got out of his car and walked back towards the track. A marshal attempted to lead him to safety but found himself the undeserving recipient of a right hook. Hunt immediately apologised but, still raging, shook his fist at the hapless Mass every time the German drove past.

Hunt was fined $2000 for walloping the marshal and $750 for walking back to the pits in an unsafe manner.

Ironically, had the two McLarens not collided then it's probable that they would have finished first and second, as the engine in Andretti's Lotus expired (for the umpteenth time that season) with three laps to run.

S9

What caused Gerhard Berger to retire from the 1995 Italian Grand Prix?

B.   His suspension was broken by a stray camera

The two Ferraris were very much in contention for victory at Monza in 1995, even before Damon Hill inadvertently took both himself and Michael Schumacher out of the race when lapping Taki Inoue.

With Coulthard having previously retired, the Ferraris were now running first and second, with Berger ahead. Alesi's pit stop was, however, quicker than that of Berger, and he emerged as the leader as the race entered its second half.

As the Ferrari duo barrelled down the main straight on lap 32, the rear-facing camera mounted on Alesi's car fell off and – you really couldn't make this up - bounced right into the path of Berger's sister car, breaking its left front suspension.

That left Alesi with a comfortable lead over Johnny Herbert, but as had happened the previous year, Jean's luck deserted him – a rear wheel bearing failed with eight laps to go, handing a fortunate victory to Herbert.

S10

Who failed to qualify for, retired, and was disqualified from the same race?

B.   Hans Heyer

Hans Heyer's date with F1 destiny came at the 1977 German Grand Prix. A very accomplished saloon car racer, Heyer jumped at the chance to drive for the German-based ATS team in his home Grand Prix.

Although he missed out on qualifying for the race, the rules of the day allowed drivers who had failed to qualify to prepare for the race, lest a driver or drivers who had qualified be unable to take the start.

When the race started, Heyer's enthusiasm got the better of him and he zoomed off after the field from the pit lane. His actions either went unnoticed or were ignored, for he was allowed to continue to race. He retired after 9 laps with gear linkage problems and was finally disqualified after the race had finished.

Heyer's actions were, however, far from unprecedented: Harald Ertl joined in the 1976 French GP after failing to qualify, and there are several other examples of it happening in previous years. Things were different then.

Surely Not II

S11

Who declined to write the foreword for the Autocourse annual?

A.   Ayrton Senna

It had been the tradition since 1963 that the new world champion would write the foreword for that year's Autocourse annual. Indeed, Senna had done so after winning the world championship in 1988.

After winning the championship in 1990, it was therefore expected that he would do so again. This time, however, he declined.

On the face of it, it seems that he was unhappy that the publication had rated Prost as the best F1 driver in 1990*. Under normal circumstances, that may not have bothered Senna to such an extent, but it came at a time when he was somewhat rankled by what he felt was unfair treatment in relation to both his disqualification from the 1989 Japanese Grand Prix and the decision by FISA not to permit him, as pole position holder, to start from the clean side of the grid at Suzuka in 1990. In Senna's eyes, Prost had unfairly benefited from both decisions, hence his irritation at being placed below the Frenchman in the Autocourse ratings.

Given Senna's declinature, the foreword was instead written by Nobuhiko Kawamoto, the CEO of Honda. Normal service was resumed the following year when Senna, who had again won the world championship, wrote the foreword.

*It was not uncommon for Autocourse's writers to pick someone other than the world champion as the year's best driver. A pertinent example of this was 1993, when Senna, who finished second to Prost in that season's championship, was rated as the year's best driver.

S12

Why was Adrian Newey 'asked to leave' Repton School?

C.   He damaged centuries-old stained glass windows

By Adrian Newey's own admission, his time at Repton was littered with a series of minor misdemeanours.

The final straw came when progressive rock band Greenslade played a student-organised gig in Pears Hall, a school building dating from the 11th century which had equally venerable stained-glass windows.

During the concert, the band's sound engineer briefly left the mixing desk unattended. This was the cue for Newey, who by his own admission had been drinking soft drinks laced with spirits, to turn up all the sliders on the mixing desk to maximum. The immediate result was a veritable wall of sound which subsided only when the sound engineer returned to the desk.

The second, and for Newey the most damning, consequence of his actions was that the explosion of sound caused by his meddling had caused damage to the stained-glass windows.

At 16, Newey's time at Repton was over.

After Repton, Newey went to the Leamington Spa College of Further Education. He did not sit A levels but instead gained an Ordinary National Diploma in Engineering. Armed with this, he gained a place at Southampton University to study Aeronautics and Astronautics. Newey excelled in his studies, gaining a First Class Honours degree and thereafter embarking on a career that would bring him fame, fortune and success.

S13

Why was F1 team owner Rob Walker banned from flying in the 1930s?

A.   He used a plane to jump the fences on a racecourse

There's lot that could be said about Rob Walker. Born into a wealthy family – his grandfather was the managing director of Johnnie Walker, he was able to indulge his passion for motor racing.

He raced fairly often in the pre-war period, finishing eighth (with co-driver Ian Connell) in the 1939 Le Mans 24 Hours, his sense of style being such that he drank a glass of champagne every time he made a pit stop.

It was, however, one of Walker's other passions that caused him to get into hot water. Having flown to a race meeting, he decided to enliven the lunch break by jumping the fences in his Tiger Moth. Unfortunately for him, his plane's registration was noted by a policeman, who duly reported him to the Air Ministry. As a result, his flying licence was revoked.

He flew again, though, as a pilot in the Fleet Air Arm during World War 2. Thereafter, he returned to motorsport, but as a team owner rather than a driver.

From 1958 until 1970, Walker's team was a regular entrant in Grands Prix, becoming the first team to win a Grand Prix with a car that it had not built. The team would go on to rack up eight further Grand Prix wins, all of them with 'customer' cars – a record that stands to this day.

S14

Who lapped Watkins Glen 9.5 seconds faster than anyone in a wet practice session in 1979?

C.   Gilles Villeneuve

Situated in upstate New York, Watkins Glen didn't always enjoy the best weather when the F1 circus arrived there every October.

This was particularly true in 1979, when the heavens opened on the Friday. Indeed, the rain was so heavy that only six cars ventured onto the track for the timed session that afternoon. The two Ferraris of Scheckter and Villeneuve were amongst that bold half-dozen.

By his own admission, Scheckter, the new world champion, scared himself silly in that session. Having pushed hard, he returned to the pits thinking that no-one could have gone faster than he had. He was wrong – Villeneuve had beaten his time. This on its own would have come as a surprise to no-one, as the French-Canadian's skill and speed were not in doubt. However, the margin by which Villeneuve had gone fastest raised more than a few eyebrows.

Scheckter's fastest time was 2 minutes 11.089 seconds, which most observers considered a fine effort in the conditions. Villeneuve had, however, gone round in 2 minutes 01.437 seconds, over nine and a half seconds faster than Scheckter, and in an identical car on identical tyres. For the avoidance of doubt, Scheckter's time put him second to his team-mate on the time sheets...

Villeneuve won the race, too. In a wet-dry race, he and Alan Jones, in the brilliant Williams FW07, simply ran away from the field. When Jones retired after a botched pit stop, Villeneuve led the race by over a lap. It was just as well that he had such a margin, as his engine's oil pressure started to fall with 25 laps to go. But, having reduced his pace by as much as 5 seconds a lap to preserve his engine, Villeneuve made it to the finish, still with nearly 50 seconds in hand over Arnoux in second place.

S15

In which year did the drivers who finished first and second in the world championship never both finish a Grand Prix in podium positions?

B.   1950

The inaugural world championship saw Nino Farina win the world championship by three points from Juan Manuel Fangio. Each man won three of the six races they both contested (neither man drove in the season's seventh race, the Indianapolis 500) but not once did they both finish a Grand Prix in a podium position.

This scenario would have been repeated in 1997, had not Michael Schumacher been excluded from the standings as punishment for his botched attempt to punt Villeneuve off the track in the final race of the season, the European Grand Prix at Estoril.

There were seventeen Grands Prix in 1997, and Schumacher and Villeneuve raced in all of them. From round four onwards, only one or the other of them led the championship, which makes the fact that they somehow managed to avoid meeting on the podium throughout the season all the more remarkable.

S16

At which circuit could 'The Bog', an area infamous for spectator misbehaviour be found?

D.   Watkins Glen

In F1 terms, the Glen was the epicentre of rowdy behaviour in the early 1970s. Hordes of people would turn up, many with little or no interest in Formula 1, and spend the race weekend in full-on party mode. There were fights, streakers, people wearing hats made out of melons, contests involving varying degrees of, er, exuberant behaviour...and then there was The Bog.

Situated outside the short straight linking turns 10 and 11, The Bog was an area of ground that was open to spectators. Nothing extraordinary about that, you might think, but by October and the Glen's annual date with F1, the rain that was no stranger to upstate New York turned the stream that ran through it into a muddy hole: The Bog.

Large numbers of racegoers flocked to The Bog. Known as Bogladytes, these hardy characters would often camp or sleep in their cars on the drier ground that lay above The Bog. For some, however, the challenge of riding their motorbike or driving their car through The Bog was just too tempting. Not all of those who took on the challenge made it, however, and more than a few cars and bikes ended their days stuck in the mud, whereupon the Bogladytes treated the stricken vehicle to a Viking funeral.

Some people even took cars, motorbikes and engines to the Glen just so that they could be sacrificed to The Bog. "The Bog wants a car", the Bogladytes would cry, and someone's means of transport would be driven or dragged into The Bog and torched.

Added to this penchant for destruction was a voracious appetite for alcohol and other stimulants, vicious games of 'the other side sucks', wet t-shirt contests, mooning, streaking (sometimes on the track itself) and an atmosphere in which rocks, bottles and sometimes even Molotov cocktails were thrown.

For years nothing much was done about the goings-on at The Bog. But then came the events of 1974. Keen to watch Emerson Fittipaldi clinch his second world championship, a group of Brazilian fans chartered a Greyhound bus to take them on the return trip between JFK airport and Watkins Glen.

Unfortunately, the bus was left unlocked and unattended, and (apparently) with the keys still in the ignition. This was just too tempting for a small group of Bogladytes, who sneaked into the bus and drove it to The Bog, slamming into parked cars on the way. Once at The Bog, the fate of the bus was sealed. Under a hail of rocks, bottles and whatever else was to hand, it was driven into The Bog and quickly set ablaze by a volley of Molotov cocktails.

An assortment of cars, at least a dozen of them, was then sacrificed to The Bog as the madness continued throughout the night.

This time, however, the Bogladytes had gone too far. By the time of the 1975 Grand Prix, the stream had been covered over and the area flattened. The Bog was no more. It didn't bring a complete halt to the partying that was part of the Glen experience, but the parties were somewhat tamer affairs from then on.

S17

Which of the following drivers missed a Grand Prix, having been suspended by his own team?

B.   Ayrton Senna

On the face of it, Ayrton Senna's contract with the Toleman F1 team was for three years. The young Brazilian had, however, been smart enough to ensure that it included a clause that would enable him to leave the team in the event that he received a better offer from another team.

So when Lotus decided that Senna was the man for them, they wasted little time in signing up him up for the following season. There was, however, one snag: the break clause in Senna's contract stipulated that he had to inform the Toleman team before accepting an offer from another team, and he had not done so.

To say that Alex Hawkridge, the Team Principal of Toleman, was unhappy about this would be an understatement. He knew that he couldn't keep a driver who wanted to go elsewhere, but he could at least register his and the team's displeasure. This he did by suspending Senna for the Italian Grand Prix.

Senna returned to the cockpit of the TG184 for the final two races of the season, taking third place in the season-ending Portuguese Grand Prix. It would the team's final podium in F1.

S18

What did Nelson Piquet do immediately after retiring from the 1982 German Grand Prix?

B.   Assault the driver with whom he had collided

The 1982 German Grand Prix is remembered for several things: Didier Pironi's career-ending accident in a very wet practice session, Patrick Tambay taking an emotional win driving a Ferrari that bore the racing number of his great friend, Gilles Villeneuve, and erstwhile race leader Nelson Piquet's post-collision attack on Eliseo Salazar.

Pironi's time in the earlier, dry qualifying session was good enough for pole position, but with the Frenchman in hospital with severe leg injuries it was decided to leave the pole position slot on the grid vacant. With Hockenheim being a power circuit, the absence of Pironi meant that victory would almost certainly go to one of the remaining five turbocharged cars on the grid. And so it proved, with Piquet's short-fuelled Brabham taking the lead and scampering off into the distance.

The Brazilian would not, however, make it as far as his planned stop to refill his fuel tank. On the eighteenth tour, he lapped Eliseo Salazar on the approach to the *Ostkurve* chicane. Unfortunately, Salazar left his braking too late, and as Piquet cut across to take the racing line the rear left wheel of his car was struck by the front right wheel of Salazar's ATS. This caused Piquet's car to hit the tyre barriers at the exit of the chicane. Both cars retired from the race on the spot.

Salazar had no sooner climbed out of the cockpit of his stricken ATS than he was confronted by the enraged Piquet. He was still wearing his crash helmet when Piquet punched and pushed him to the head. The Brazilian threw in an attempted kick for good measure, but this particular effort missed the mark. Salazar made no attempt to retaliate.

When Piquet later learned that his engine had issues that would have caused it to expire before the end of the race, he telephoned Salazar and apologised to him.

The race was won by Ferrari's Patrick Tambay. It was his first Grand Prix victory and it came in only his fourth race for Ferrari after replacing Gilles Villeneuve, who had died in a crash at Zolder in Belgium. With Pironi now also out for the season (his injuries were such that he never returned to Formula One), Tambay now found himself as Ferrari's lead driver for the rest of the season.

One final point: Pironi's career-ending crash resulted from his Ferrari ploughing into the back of Alain Prost's Renault at high speed as a result of spray obscuring his vision. Prost went to the aid of Pironi and witnessed the appalling injuries to his countryman's legs. It is said that Prost's dislike of racing in very wet conditions stemmed from that day.

S19

In which 1967 Grand Prix did Jim Clark re-take the lead after losing a lap due to a puncture?

A.   Italy

Having started from pole position, Jim Clark soon found himself part of a four-way slipsteaming battle for the lead in the early stages of the 1967 Italian Grand Prix. On lap 13, however, a puncture caused him to lose a lap. What thereafter followed was one of the greatest drives of his career.

He rejoined the circuit over a lap down on the leading group, which was comprised of his Lotus team-mate Graham Hill and the Brabhams of Denny Hulme and Jack Brabham.

Clark rapidly caught the leading group and unlapped himself. He thereafter started to work his way back up through the field. As the field started to spread out, Hulme dropped out of the race and Hill broke free of Brabham. By this time, Clark's pace was such that he was now lapping over two seconds faster than Brabham. Indeed, his fastest race lap equalled his pole position time.

On lap 59, the engine in Hill's Lotus expired. That left Brabham leading from Surtees and the rapidly closing Clark. On lap 61, Clark passed Brabham and re-took the lead that he'd lost a little over an hour before. On the 68th and last lap, however, the fuel pump in Clark's Lotus malfunctioned, almost bringing him to a halt at the *Curva Grande* and making him easy prey for both Brabham and Surtees. With his engine coughing and spluttering, he managed to limp home in third place, scant reward for a superb drive.

With Clark out of contention, it was between Surtees and Brabham for the win. In the end, Surtees took victory by 0.2 seconds. It was his sixth and final Grand Prix victory and it was achieved in the first Grand Prix for the new Honda RA300. It wasn't enough to keep Honda in F1, however, and the Japanese team withdrew at the end of the season.

S20

Which driver took part in a powerboat race wearing a gorilla outfit to hide his identity?

B.   Kimi Raikkonen

In the summer of 2007, Kimi and a couple of friends entered a powerboat race at Hanko, Finland...dressed in gorilla suits. They didn't win the race but did take home a trophy for being the best-dressed crew.

It wasn't the first time, however, that the Iceman had taken part in some extra-curricular racing. Earlier that year, he entered a snowmobile race in

Finland under the name, 'James Hunt', circumventing any problems about obtaining permission from Ferrari to take part in the race by neglecting to tell them about it.

He won that snowmobile race and followed it up by taking victory in the season-opening Australian Grand Prix before going on to score five more Grand Prix wins and win the world championship.

Five years later, he again paid tribute to James Hunt, a man whose company Kimi would undoubtedly have enjoyed, by wearing a replica of Hunt's crash helmet in practice and qualifying for the 2012 Monaco Grand Prix.

About The Authors

David M. Milloy (writer)

David practised law for over twenty years before escaping from the legal profession in order to fulfil a childhood ambition by becoming a motoring writer.

Since changing career, David has written for a number of publications in both printed and digital media, including Classic Car Weekly, Absolute Lotus and Influx.

He's been a fan of F1 since childhood, though his own racing ambitions never made it past the stage of being only moderately rubbish at Scalextric. He thought he knew quite a lot about F1 before researching material for this book; he now realises that he was wrong about that!

Marcus T. Ward (illustrations)

Living in Staffordshire not too far away from the Cheshire and Shropshire borders, Marcus is a digital artist mostly using the Affinity Designer drawing package.

Whilst recuperating from a back injury in early 2018, he decided to attempt to take up drawing to ease his boredom. He draws in a variety of styles from simple illustrative drawings to near life-like works.

Trained in electronics and software engineering, the only previous drawing experience was CAD work designing printed circuit boards and industrial rechargeable battery packs.

Marcus will admit to being stuck in a time bubble due to his interest and love of 1960's & 1970's rock music and cars.

Printed in Great Britain
by Amazon